WHEN THE SCORPION

WHEN THE SCORPION

a play in four acts

Onyechi Mbamali

authorHOUSE®

AuthorHouse™ UK Ltd.
1663 Liberty Drive
Bloomington, IN 47403 USA
www.authorhouse.co.uk
Phone: 0800.197.4150

Published by AuthorHouse   11/21/2013

ISBN: 978-1-4567-9209-1 (sc)
ISBN: 978-1-4567-9210-7 (e)

Inspired by

the early Christian missionaries here in Africa
their pioneering spirit and lifework
undimmed by age, still largely unsung.

Cast

Abednego . . . .*Warrant Chief Designate*

Sergeant
Lance Corporal   } *Policemen*
Three Constables

Oyidi'a . . . . *The king's widow*

Akaeze . . . . *Traditional Prime Minister*

Orimili Obiora . . . . *High Chief*

Ugochi . . . . *princess, Obiora's wife*

Ojongo . . . . *Juju Priest*

Ebili . . . . *Village drunk*

Echezo . . . . *Head of palace atttendants*

Akweke . . . . *Local belle*

Kiki
Zizzi   } *City belles*
Pimpim
Iquo

Ogbuefi Iwobi . . . . *Titled man*

Four sons of Iwobi

Daughters of Iwobi (Uzoma and two others)

Five elders *in Iwobi's trance*

Rev Jones . . . . a white preacher gunned down

Ogbuefi Ekwegbalu . . . . *Titled man*

Okpijo . . . . A thug

Pregnant woman

Three women at early dawn

A woman and her four-year old son

Armed Guards

Layabouts

Country elders

Ajofia's ghost *in Iwobi's trance*

PROLOGUE

Total black-out on stage. A woman's voice wails a deep long lament, her sobs and choked cries punctuated with tear-soaked words

An evil gun, an evil gun
An evil gun has killed a man
Killed an innocent man
A stranger who came to us
A good man who sang to us
A visitor who laughed with us
An evil gun has shot him dead
Shot him dead
Shot him dead . . . .
A stranger who came to us
A white man's son, I'm lost

> *[Spotlight falls on the heavily pregnant sobbing woman, sprawled out on the empty stage]*

People, we are lost
Umudimkpa, our country
We are finished
Like Umuachala, finished
The white man's anger
Fires and loaded guns
More graves in courtyards
Than mounds in farmlands
Is that our need, is that our prayer?
Egbuna, my brother
What made you do this deed?
If you forgot everything

Must you forget your own name?
Egbuna, your birth name, a prayer
That you must do no murder
Do no murder. Egbuna.
Did the elders foresee this day?
Who foresees tomorrow's child . . . .

> *[Two male voices are heard in discussion off-stage.*
> *She strains her ears and rises in slow degrees]*

1st Voice: Will crying bring him back . . . or tears save a mourner? If he is dead, he is dead . . . .

2nd Voice: No chance of survival. He took the shot straight in the chest, and he lost too much blood!

1st Voice: Then, it is a race for dear life. Every rat to the bush, every lizard to the road! White man's anger, guns of evil!

1st Voice: Guns of evil and mass graves! This is Egbuna's war!

> *[The woman frets, casts about in fright. Lights*
> *fade as she skitters from stage . . . . . . Blackout]*

Act 1, Scene 1

Late night, in the Throne Room at Umudimkpa Palace. All seats are vacant and stand in a half-moon—the king's imposing throne in the middle, the queen's stool sharing a minor part of the dais with it, and the seven stools of the high chiefs lined out on both flanks on the scrubbed mud floor. Standing on the front edge of the dais and backing the throne is a crude wooden desk with two empty cane chairs, one behind it, the other at its head. Abednego, pipe in mouth and full of airs, chats with Sergeant at the entrance.

Abednego: Too few, Sergeant! Only five captured? That's too few!

                        [He moves towards the dais, Sergeant following respectfully]

Sergeant *[solicitously]:*   We will capture all before dawn; for sure, O king.

Abednego: You will kill every one of them.

Sergeant: No, king! We are not allowed to kill anybody in our custody.

Abednego: That's a famous lie! You must kill them off. No nanny cry!

Sergeant: We need court orders then.

Abednego: Court orders take too long. Why waste resources on idiots who are going to die? They eat too much, plus they occupy much space, plus they take the fresh air that better people need for longer life! Keeping them is stupid and mere pretence. As your king, I forbid it.

Sergeant:	But king . . . .
Abednego:	Kill them off, I say. Make vultures happy or bush dogs! Fair is fair.
Sergeant *[thoughtfully]:*	But only the court can condemn a man to death . . . . That is the white man's law, O king.
Abednego:	Never you quote the law at me. That is very offensive! Don't be rude!
Sergeant:	Pardon me, O king, but this is one rule the white man shouts and shouts till he turns red in the face!
Abednego:	The same white man has made me king in this place. Paramount ruler is who I am. Do you even understand the size of my power?
Sergeant:	King, I don't mean to argue but . . . .
Abednego:	I can do what I want any way I want it. Nobody in the kingdom can stop me. I am bigger than the court of law. If you have a head on your neck, never argue with me. Argument is stupid; I hate it from you. Find common sense; wipe out those worms! That is an order.
Sergeant:	We have to be careful O king. It is my honest advice. We need to be very, very careful.
Abednego:	Watch your tongue! You are talking to the paramount ruler of all Umudimkpa. How dare you ask me to be careful?
Sergeant:	It is wisdom I'm urging O king.
Abednego:	It is fear I see in your eyes. If you can't do simple things my way, I'll put someone else in charge. Who put dog in *gorment* uniform?
Sergeant:	I am loyal, O king. I will always be loyal to you.
Abednego:	As if you have a choice! Do you imagine you have a choice?

Sergeant [shifting about uncomfortably]: You are the warrant chief, sir.

Abednego: Warrant what? I am Paramount Ruler!

Sergeant: Yes sir, true sir! Paramount ruler! The king, sir!

                                [Abednego mounts the dais, stands near the table]

Abednego: I can remove you anytime. If you fail me just once, I tell D.O. straight; *fiam!* that uniform is off your back and you go back as nothing-nothing to the nothing village from where you came! Let that wisdom dwell in your ears always.

Sergeant [saluting nervously]: Yes sir! Shon sir!

                                [Enter Lance Corporal, salutes]

Lance Corporal: The men are ready for us, sir. We shall escort the king.

Abednego: How many guards?

Lance Corporal: Six and fully armed, sir.

Sergeant: Not sir. This is king. Say king! Always say king!

Lance Corporal: Yes sir! King sir!

Sergeant: Six armed men, O king.

Abednego: Make it ten for me. The king cannot walk that distance to the camp with only six guards. This is a dark and dangerous night. You must think in the head always.

Sergeant [saluting]:   We must find ten men, sir, King! Go arrange it, Corp'l.

Lance Corp'l: Yes sir . . . . King sir! [salutes, Exits]

Abednego: Think in the head, Sergeant. What does D.O. want from me?

Sergeant: He did not tell me O king. He only said [immitating the airs and accent of an Englishman *rather poorly]* "Sergeant, go quickly. Tell king to see me quickly."

[Abednego draws one of the chairs from beside the desk and sits down, puffing on his pipe]

Abednego: Always think in your head! We all moved to that camp after the shooting. Why did he send me back to this palace?

Sergeant *[scratching his head in thought]:* Because . . . you are king!

Abednego: I am king anywhere I am. The king in me is king everywhere! Think in your head.

Sergeant: I'm thinking, O King. I'm thinking very hard.

Abednego: You're not using your brains. That's very bad, Sergeant. And your head is big . . . . like a coconut of the shrine!

Sergeant: No complaint sir, King.

Abednego: Everything is brains, Sergeant! Not the size of an empty head! D.O. wants a thinking man and a strong man. So he chose me.

Sergeant: He made the best choice O king. You have a great head . . . . a thinking head I mean, sir.

Abednego: I have the brains. I can face all the trouble in this country for the white man. Even the trouble of spirit land!

Segeant: That is true, sir.

Abednego: If anybody gives me a headache, instant finish! Who *born* dog!

Sergeant: You have all powers, king. You are the paramount ruler, sir.

Abednego: My people are scatter-heads but D.O. is too much for them. He is thinking in his head like "You bushmen, you killed my brother; now, kill your own brother!" Very clever is white man!

	Very clever! He put me here to fight my own brothers for him.
Sergeant:	It is war, O king.
Abednego:	A war which I must win! I know D.O. He will remain in the camp and never near this palace until I win the peace for him.
Sergeant:	You are right O king.
Abednego:	I am always right. D.O. himself knows well . . . But why he is calling me now is what I cannot explain. What does he want?
Sergeant:	I'm not sure, O King. But I am thinking . . . . and it may not be wrong if . . . . I guess probably he wants to hear something . . . . like what the king is doing maybe . . . . I am not very sure about it . . . . but perhaps . . . it is something about . . . security, I think!
Abednego:	Correct, Sergeant! You see? You are not as daft as you look!
Sergeant:	Thank you, king.
Abednego:	True talk! Even that stupid look on your face can become a big advantage . . . . . . and we can use it when necessary. It depends.
Sergeant [eagerly]:	How sir? How can I make it sir?
Abednego:	Stupidity has its own uses, Sergeant. If you impress me on this job, I will teach you many valuable secrets. That is the advantage of working for me! I make people think in the head always, but first you must impress me; only those who impress me can join my inner circle.
Sergeant:	I will impress sir. I will press and impress. I will even compress. You will like how I work, sir. You will see my hand, sir. King sir.

Abednego:	Calm down, Sergeant. Calm down. Step by step!
Sergeant:	Yes, king. Shon sir! Step by step, sir.
Abednego:	First step, Sergeant . . . . Narrate to me now, everything we did about security. Everything, point by point!
Sergeant:	Point by point sir! We arrested the two high chiefs, Akaeze and Orimili.
Abednego:	Are you forgetting the one called Mmanko, the kidnap chief?
Sergeant:	D.O. is taking that one to Ubulu, to try him there and hang him.
Abednego:	Correct. Next?
Sergeant:	We also arrested the woman they call High Mother.
Abednego:	Correct. Her titled name is Oyidi'a. Call it.
Sergeant:	Oyidi'a.
Abednego:	What next?
Sergeant:	We arrested the old one called Ochilizi.
Abednego:	Oche-ilo-eze.
Sergeant:	Oche . . .
Abednego:	Don't be deceived by his age. He is a very dangerous man.
Sergeant:	We suspected that.
Abednego:	Don't just suspect; keep a close eye on him. Otherwise, somebody's entire front teeth will be whacked off!
Sergeant:	In that case, O King, can we tie him up like a mad bull too?
Abednego:	Don't wait to be told everything. Your work is state security! The king is the kingdom and his

personal security is the security of all. Think in the head always, Sergeant.

Sergeant:	All correct, sir. King sir! Shon sir! Straight security!
Abednego:	Who else have you arrested?
Sergeant:	We have the danger boy, the one called Egbuna. He is the man who killed the white priest.
Abednego:	That one is our most important prisoner. Where is he now?
Sergeant:	We are keeping him in the tightest corner in this very palace.
Abednego:	I've warned you times and numbers. That boy is *gorment's* enemy number one. He must not escape.
Sergeant:	King, he is tied up like an evil beast and four men are guarding him! King sir, if you see the ropes on his hands and feet, their strength can pull the chief of elephants together with his wives and concubines, home and abroad, joined as one!
Abednego:	Don't let me hear a stupid story how cockroach ate iron and the fat mouse slipped away.
Sergeant:	King, sir, I was there to check everything by myself. The sharpest matchet in the whole world cannot cut that rope!
Abednego:	My ears have heard. What else have you done?
Sergeant:	We have captured five members of Gosiora and Osilike. Those are the two evil cults that drank a terrible oath to wipe out the white man and all his people—which is us.
Abednego:	Those boys are very dangerous, very, very dangerous. Not a single one of them should be

left alive or nobody in this land can sleep with two eyes. You must catch them this night!

Sergeant: They are small rats, king . . . We shall pick everyone of them up.

Abednego: They killed three policemen and took their guns. I want those guns back before daybreak to present them to D.O. in person!

Sergeant: I will deliver the guns to you, O King.

Abednego: If you fail, *fiam!* Off you go. No time for nanny cry!

[*Re-enter Lance Corporal, nervously. Stands at attention*]

Sergeant: O King, ten guards are ready for you, sir.

Lance Corporal [*nervously*]: But there is bad news, sir. I don't know how to say it.

Sergeant: What happened? What has happened?

Lance Corporal: I was not the one, sir . . . But I have to say it to you. I don't know how it happened, sir. But . . . but . . . . it has happened again, sir.

Sergeant: What happened again?

Lance Corporal: Yes sir, they said it . . . . But I was not there when it happened.

Sergeant: So what happened?

Lance Corporal: Even where it happened I was not there. They came . . . and that is how I heard it, sir . . . . they told me, sir.

Sergeant: Told you what? Talk like a policeman!

Lance Corporal: They say another one has happened, sir.

Abednego: Another what, you idiot? Open your mouth!

Lance Corporal: King, it is another policeman.

Sergeant: Another policeman. What?

Lance Corporal: They killed him . . . . and they took his gun, sir.

Abednego [*flies in wild rage across the hall*]: Sergeant! Ser-gea-nt! That makes it four! Four, Sergeant! Four, four! What do you want me to tell D.O.? You and your men are useless! Useless! What am I to tell D.O.?

Sergeant: King, we cannot tell D.O.

Abednego: What do you mean, you idiot?

Sergeant [*turning furiously on the Lance Corporal*]: Go away, you idiot! Let me talk to king in private!

Abednego: Four policemen!

[*He slowly returns to his chair . . . Exit Lance Corporal*]

Sergeant: King, we cannot near D.O. with four policemen are dead.

Abednego: You're a fool! The white man has ears to hear things for himself. He will hear before dawn.

Sergeant: King, we can make a story for his ears. We can say that all the people who killed policemen have been arrested.

Abednego: You're an idiot! You think the white man is a fool like you? He will ask me to show him the arrested men.

Sergeant: That is not a problem, King. We are arresting a lot of men. They cannot speak white man's language.

Abednego [*ponders awhile*]: So?

Sergeant [*shrugging*]: So, O king.

Abednego [*ponders more, smiles*]: Ahaaa! I see your nose. I see you very well. We can accuse anyone we choose of anything we choose!

Sergeant:	Even when someone is innocent, what can he say for himself? Whatever he says in our language, we put what we like into the ears of the white man!
Abednego *[laughs aloud]*:	Sarge! This is nice. This is very nice. I said it before and I was right. Always right. You are not as stupid as you look.
Sergeant:	Thank you O King.
Abednego:	See to it then. Arrest many more people. Anyone who looks like trouble or smells like one, arrest them all.
Sergeant:	Thank you, my King.
Abednego:	Now we can go and see D.O. Men with guns all around me!
Sergeant:	Shon sir! All correct, sir!
Abednego:	When we come back, I begin to sit on this throne. Practice makes perfect. I am king of Umudimkpa!
Sergeant:	Shon sir! All correct sir! But King, sir . . .
Abednego:	Yes, Sergeant?
Sergeant:	I fear something . . . . like . . . . another big problem!
Abednego:	What again, Sergeant?
	[Sergeant removing his cap, scratches his head nervously]
Sergeant:	King, sir . . . . They say . . . . it is going to be death. That is what I hear; that it will be death . . . if somebody sits on this throne . . . Too many bad things are being said about this throne!
Abednego:	It is an ancient throne . . . . the power of many generations. Only someone strong and special can sit on it. Who else but me?

Sergeant:	King, your people are saying that you won't even try . . . . They say you will die the very instant your body touches the throne.
Abednego:	I am Paramount Ruler . . . . That is what D.O. himself has called me. Ruler Paramount! I will choose for myself where to sit.
Sergeant:	Wisdom will be your seat, O king. I can see that the people of this country, they are not wise at all! They don't know it is their good luck that you agreed to become their king.
Abednego:	Never mind the ingrates! They are all idiots. Most of them don't like my face . . . . but what is that to me? I am king over them all . . . . Let it pain them deep in the head and let them run into the bush to hang themselves! My feet have entered this palace! I shall wear a royal crown and sit on this throne no matter what anybody cooks in his soup pot! Let's go, Sergeant.

[Exeunt Abednego and Sergeant]

[Fade]

Act 1, Scene 2

Throne Room at Umudimkpa palace. Enter Constable 1, looks around the palace, then claps his hands in a signal to someone at the door.

Constable 1:
You can bring him in.

[Enter Constables 2 and 3 shoving Ebili forward. He is swaying drunkenly, his large calabash dangling from a rope over his shoulder]

Ebili *[swaying drunkenly]*:
I know that man better than you all. I knew him from infancy and that's the truth. That's the truth. He and I were childhood playmates.

Constable 1:
You see yourself? Your age mate went far away and achieved wonders; but you stuck yourself in this village like a native pot that fetches nothing year in, year out. Look at yourself . . . . Envy of King Abednego the Great is now killing you!

Ebili:
I can tell you truths about that man! His name is not even that thing you call him.

Constable 3:
Shut up your mouth!

Ebili:
Shut up my mouth? The night that lends cover to a vile serpent will find out later. Even in the dark, venom is truth!

Constable 1:
Truth! Truth! Every sentence, Truth! Who cares about truth?

Constable 3:
The whole world is tired of truths that make people unhappy.

Ebili:	The whole world is sick of liars and false witnesses. It is a sad night in this palace.
Constable 1:	Only fools choose complaints as necklaces, sadness as apparel. What do you stand to gain, railing like a madman at what you cannot change? Abednego the Great is king of Umudimkpa!
Ebili:	You keep calling that name. It is not the fellow's name!
Constable 3:	He is King Abednego the First, the great pillar of power, friend of the white man and paramount ruler of all Umudimkpa.
Ebili:	He is Apiti, the dirty mud under my feet.
Constable 1:	Shut up your mouth!
Constable 2:	Why do you insult the king of your country?
Ebili:	Don't make me laugh. Apiti, king? Tcha! Whose king? That fellow is a vagabond and a criminal!

[Constable 1 slaps him hard in the face]

Constable 3:	That serves you right! Loud Mouth!
Ebili:	Another mistake. Another big mistake!
Constable 1:	Whose mistake, you drunkard? Yours or mine?
Ebili *[reeling]*:	Stars are dancing in my eyes . . . My head is shooting guns at my head . . . . I need to sit me down somewhere . . . Was it a question you asked or me? See . . . what was I telling you? a million slaps . . . . that's what I said it . . . . ten million slaps cannot stop the truth.
Constable 1 *[angrily]*:	You are still mouthing truth, truth, truth. Time we saw the truth of your own life!

[He wrestles the calabash from Ebili and raises it with both hands above his head. Ebili sobers up instantly]

Ebili *[pleading]*:	Ah please, please, ple-e-ease! Don't do that one, don't . . .
Constable 1 *[mocking]*:	So what is the truth now, your pot or your grief?
Ebili:	Please don't do it. She's innocent, nothing to do with king or palace, she's my life companion, she's really . . . . Ask anybody . . . See, I'm not drunk any more! My eyes are now clear . . . . No please, no! No-o-o!

> *[Constable 1 ignoring the plea, smashes the calabash on the floor. All three laugh, dancing around Ebili. He squats on the floor grieving, gathers the bits and pieces]*

Constable 2:	This is what happens to the enemies of the king!
Constable 3:	They will be broken in pieces. Orders are orders!
Constable 1:	They will cry in dark holes and no one will hear them.
Constable 2:	They will crawl on their bellies like amputee insects.
Constable 3:	Orders are orders! We shall create fear in this kingdom!
Constable 2:	Fear in every heart, fear in every head!
Constable 3:	We shall amputate every cockroach that refuses to mind his own business. Orders are orders!
Constable 1:	We are the special arm of the king!
Constable 3:	his secret power to shatter and scatter! We can do the never-done! Orders are orders!
Constable 2:	Anyone who troubles the king is dead in our hands.

Constable 3:   We shall be ruthless! Way forward, allow no trouble to start!

Constable 2:   With cat nose, smell mischief from a far distance.

Constable 3:   Kill without pity once there is suspicion!

Constable 1 *[uncomfortably]:* That is the bit that actually worries me . . . . Why should we kill a human being on mere suspicion?

Constable 3:   What is the worry, an evil child in the womb of his mother? Orders are to kill instantly. So far no one sees our hand in it!

Constable 2:   But how can we know a bad child in the womb of his mother?

Constable 3:   When in doubt, kill mother and child! Orders are orders!

     [Constable 1 fetches a broom, casts it down at Ebili's feet]

Constable 1:   Sweep!

Constable 2:   He's still shedding floods of tears . . . . for a common calabash?

Constable 3:   Suppose we'd broken your skull instead? We can still do that; no challenge.

     [Ebili rises slowly to his feet, the shards in his open hands]

Ebili *[remotely]:* The wicked have finally done their worst.

Constable 3:   If you call us wicked, we do you wicked. We are in power!

Ebili *[sinks to his knees again, grieving deeply]:* She was true love . . . Always there for me . . . My precious love is gone!

Constable 3 *[to all]:* This is ridiculous! Wasn't that just a calabash?

Ebili [*to the shards in his hands*]: A fellow man wrecks my joy and mocks my tears . . . . But, you are my firstlove; no one can take your place.

> [*He rises, lays the shards gently on the floor at a corner*]

Constable 3: I said it from the onset, this fellow is mad in the head; but you both say he's only drunk. Is this not a final proof of madness?

Constable 2: Madness is a clown of a thousand masks; her ugliest she gives to over-aged infants, any adult who adores a lifeless thing as if it has a soul.

Ebili: Everything has a soul except a mob; and a mob is not numbers!

Constable 1: Everything is a mob in the eyes of a drunk!

Constable 2: Or teach us by your famous experience what else is a mob?

Ebili: Only a man who is glad to destroy what he cannot make: that is a mob. He has no soul.

> [*Constable 1 kicks the broom toward Ebili*]

Constable 1: Sweep, man!

Ebili: Not even the common beetle would make your kind of mistake; he knows the difference between hands and feet.

Constable 1: Are you crazy, man? No more of your silly jesting! Just sweep!

Ebili: Where you come from, it's like water is fetched in baskets. In Umudimkpa, not every hand touches the palace broom. [*He resists as Constable 1 tries forcing the broom into his hand*]

Constable 1: Sweep, loud mouth. I command you to sweep!

Ebili: You have killed yourself like a foolish stranger. I pity you, man.

Constable 1:	Pity yourself, you drunken millipede. Sweep or perish!
Ebili:	You are already perishing, stranger! The broom you took up is about to finish you. Don't near my body!
Constable 1:	What is wrong with this man? Take this broom from me!
Ebili:	Who wants to share death with you?
Constable 1:	You are the one about to die!
Ebili:	You are already a stark dead body; but a corpse does not mind what he wears to the grave. And he has no advisor.
Constable 1:	What is he talking about?
Ebili:	That broom in your hand. It is the anger of the gods gathered together. All the cries and curses in this kingdom . . . that's what you are carrying in your hand. It is death! Painful death!

[Constable 1 drops the broom nervously]

Constable 1:	You are bluffing.
Ebili:	Exact last words of one naughty insect who ignored his well wishers and dated a bullfrog.
Constable 1:	How dare you threaten us?
Ebili:	Am I a bullfrog?
Constable 1:	Do you imagine we are here for play?
Ebili:	What kind of play drags an innocent man all the way to the palace against his will, slaps him in the face and breaks his pot of livelihood?
Constable 1:	It's like you really need a second slap. Is that what you want?
Ebili:	The gods of this land will answer for me for this new madness that is driving you strangers to

	intolerable excesses! You now challenge the very gods as well.
Constable 1:	What is the meat of the gods with your mess on the floor?
Ebili:	You touched their sacred broom; you held the broom of the gods in your two hands and every eye saw you! You are finished, stranger!
	[Sudden silence, all regarding the broom with awe]
Constable 2:	It is a mere broom. Is it not?
Constable 3:	Nothing will happen.
Ebili:	If you believe your own self, go touch it yourself as he did.
	[All recoil from the broom]
Constable 2 *[nervously]:*	What will happen now? What do you think will happen?
Ebili:	That broom will speak. It will answer you by itself, one by one.
Constable 3:	How?
Ebili:	It will sweep out your entire families from the face of this earth. Normally, it starts with your dearest ones.
Constable 1:	Who believes such nonsense? I don't believe it.
Constable 2:	I don't either.
Ebili:	Why talk and talk and talk? Go there and pick it up!
	[All still recoil from the broom]
Constable 1:	If it had such powers, it should have stopped the white man.
Constable 3:	Yes, why didn't it get up and sweep the white man away?

Ebili:	The white man never touches a broom, does he? He's a very clever stranger; see, he uses native fools as hands and feet to do things he won't dare and take things he won't touch. You are the ones who crossed the path of the spirits. You must bear the consequences on your own heads. What is that to white man?

[The policemen visibly nervous, confer, then explode]

Constable 1:	This is nonsense.
Constable 2:	Pure nonsense!
Constable 3:	That's what white man calls jumbo jumbo.
Constable 2:	Mumbo jumbo!
Constable 1:	Who are we?
Constables 2 & 3:	We are police!
Constable 1:	Police power?
Constables 2 & 3:	Gorment power!
Constable 1:	Gorment power?
Constables 2 & 3:	No challenge!
Ebili:	Odour!
Constables 2 & 3 *[involuntarily]:*	Ye-sah!
Constable 1:	Are you mad?
Ebili:	Forgive I'm not one of you.
Constable 3:	So next time, keep quiet at a parade.
Ebili *[mimics the salute drill]:*	Ye-sah!
Constable 1:	Look. That broom cannot remain here. You have to remove it.
Ebili:	I did not put it there.
Constable 1:	But, I permit you to . . . . go and remove it.

Ebili:	Permit yourself. There is a proverb that the hand that brings an amulet must know where to keep it.
Constable 2:	Man, do you know you are still under arrest?
Ebili:	What does that mean?
Constable 2:	It means we can tie you like a goat or cage you like a dog.
Constable 3:	Or flog you like a thief.
Constable 1:	But instead, we're being nice to you, like very good friends.
Ebili:	I took a slap in the face. Friendship like that endears me completely to my worst enemies.
Constable 2:	Forget that slap. Even the best of friends fight sometimes.
Ebili:	Exactly! Friends are people who break your heart and lend you something to sweep away the broken pieces.
Constable 1:	We are only trying to do our duty. Why take it so personal?
Ebili:	Friend, a slap is a very personal thing. It gives you a private feeling that somebody owes you something.

[Ebili draws an invisible line on the floor with a big toe]

Constable 1 *[suspiciously]:*	What are you doing?
Ebili:	Separating myself and my people from the evil of that broom.

[All three policemen flock in panic to his side]

Constable 1:	We are your friends, man. Take us as friends. We only did what we were ordered to do.
Constable 2:	Brother, we did not mess with you . . . . compared with other arrests. This job is hard! You never

know someone until you try to arrest him. Wild animals are better than most people!

Constable 3:   Some people, you cannot hold them down except you break their skull or limbs! Sometimes, we have to burn down a whole house because of one stubborn goat.

Ebili: That's what worries me; the white man is up against our goats!

Constable 3:   I wasn't talking of actual goats. I meant trouble makers.

[Ebili stepping to a corner, describes circles round his head, snapping his fingers. Constables mope in fear]

Constable 1:   What are you doing?

Ebili: You are asking!

[They rush to Ebili's side and emulate his motions—squat on the floor, place both hands on the head etc]

Constable 1:   If you are blaming the white man for your trouble, your arrest has nothing to do with him.

Constable 2:   It is the king himself who ordered you arrested, along with other potential trouble makers.

Ebili: Potential trouble makers?

Constable 2:   Yes, those are people who are more trouble than the real trouble makers . . . . It came to the king's ears that you are one of them. Somebody heard you saying bad things about the king.

[A loud gunshot! The constables go flat on the floor]

Ebili: Trouble makers!

[The constables slowly pick themselves up, all nervous]

Constable 3:   That was close!

Constable 2:   Too close! I hope the men on duty know their duty!

Constable 1:   We need to be careful.

Constable 3:   Most of the guards are full of local gin!

[Ebili unperturbed, continues his motions as a second blast sends all the constables fleeing in panic]

Ebili *[with a chuckle, turns to face the wall]:*   Potential   trouble makers!

[Fade]

Act 1, Scene 3

Throne Room at the Umudimkpa palace. Ebili squatting on his haunches, faces a side wall. The three constables re-enter, looking edgy and cautious.

Constable 2: I don't believe their story at all. It is like child talk, full of holes!

Constable 3: There was no attack; no sign of any attack.

Constable 2: I think our men on duty just lost their nerves.

Constable 3: We spend time chasing jokers. But the number of idiots carrying rifles behind our backs is the big problem.

> *[Constable 1 squats beside Ebili. His two colleagues follow]*

Constable 1: My brother, you are really a nice person. I advise you to join us on the king's side!

Ebili *[rising abruptly]*: You are still saying king, king. Only the mouth of strangers can call Apiti king.

Constable 1: But king is what he is. *[Rising]* The white man has decided it.

Ebili: It is a wicked joke in our ears. Scum is a praise word if you and I are speaking of the same person.

Constables *[in unison]*: He is king!

Ebili *[laughing]*: The man you call king will never sit on this throne. Apiti is an ugly mess. The hand of the gods will sweep him out of for us!

Constable 3:	Stop! Please stop! See, I cover my ears. I cover both my ears!
Constable 2:	I too, I too! We are his men. Look, we are under oath to die for him. No dog will let you bite his master, friendship or not.
Ebili:	Are you calling yourself a dog?
Constable 3:	Watchdog . . . bodyguard . . . We must protect him from any attack!
Constable 2:	All kinds of attacks from all sides—bad words, wicked jokes everywhere! Why are these people against their own son?
Constable 3:	Foolishness I call it! Potential trouble makers everywhere!
Constable 1:	Why are good men always hated for nothing and envied for everything? And you, a nice man, why join the hate mob?
Constable 3:	Orders are orders! Any mob against the king, wipe-out!
Constable 2:	This king will reign like others whether people want him or not.
Ebili:	You are talking like this because you are complete strangers here. You don't know Apiti . . . You don't even have the faintest idea what he is. But the gods are not dead. Their broom will sweep him off with all his supporters, white or black!

[All recoil from the broom on the floor]

Constable 3 *[nervously]:*	Brother, let us stop talking about that broom.
Ebili:	If you stop talking about that man.
Constable 1:	The man is king. Can't you understand that? We have a duty to him! If you can't respect that duty, we cannot be friends.

Constable 2:	It is wisdom to befriend a king. And any king is king!
Ebilii:	This is a bad dream . . . But, I really should be laughing perhaps.
Constable 2:	What is funny?
Ebili:	Apiti, dirty mud that is a clear disgrace to all mankind . . . . First, he returns as Abanidiegwu, terror of night; then you strangers bring him into our palace, and then you call him king!
Constable 1:	Forget whatever he used to be called. He is now the *Ogbu Wala Wala,* The Killer at his own random pleasure.
Constable 2:	The *Mkpufia Aru, Obodo ana ebe,* the Bruise on the skin that makes the country cry.
Constable 3:	The *Tigbulu Enyi Tigbulu Anyinya,* The Force that pummels both elephant and horse to death.
Constable 2:	The *Tagbulu Efi Togbolu Mgbede,* The one that bites a bull to death and drops the carcass for the evening.
Ebili:	There is a sober limit to a good joke. The king of Umudimkpa is never called by such titles.
Constable 2:	That was before the white man put his foot in this palace. Umudimkpa must now wear the same rags and ribbons as all her neighbours, no difference.
	[Ebili retires to a corner bench in silence, the men following]
Constable 3:	Have you considered that the white man must avenge his brother's death?

Constable 2:	Who'd blame him? Someone here was stupid enough to take a gun and shoot a white man dead. Is that as drinking water?
Constable 1:	If that boy was born with the bad head to kill a white man, why couldn't he grow the good sense to pick his victim? Are there not gangs of red faces tormenting people here and there? Why kill a man of peace, a lamb that never offended anyone?

[Lights dim, soft breeze]

Reverend Jones was so gentle I used to think he was unreal. He was like a messenger from the world of gentle spirits. I could never understand how someone could be kind like that.

Constable 2:	He never touched a weapon of war. He even refused to allow us to bear arms coming out here with him. His death is a blow. I fear for Umudimkpa.
Constable 3:	Fear? The white man's vengeance that I saw in other lands wiped out whole villages. At Umuachala, hundreds of children became orphans and scores of young brides, instant widows!
Constable 1:	Umudimkpa has to be different. The king must save his people.
Constable 3:	If they refuse to be saved, what can he do for them? It is the foolishness of the people by the people that kills the people.
Constable 1:	Brother, join us on the king's side. It is wisdom.
Constable 3:	He even confided in us that you used to be friends. Join the winning side, man; your friend can even make you a high chief!
Ebili:	Make me a high chief? *[laughs aloud]* What daybreak for Apiti! The stench of evil to be

covered with sweet music! *[Rises. Constable 3 does same. Lights brighten]*

Constable 3: Stench . . . . Music . . . ? I don't get that.

Ebili: I shall put it more bluntly. Nobody can get me into a retinue of hired singers who hold a canopy of praise over a stinking mess!

Constable 3: Stinking mess? What are you talking about?

Ebili: Praise can never sing in a camp of evil! A stench that shuts mouths and nostrils will only draw grunts of distaste around the man you call king. That is why that broom must sweep.

Constable 1 *[frustrated, follows Ebili]*: Man, you are still under arrest. You must help us or we cannot help you any more.

Ebili *[returning to his seat]*: Help me with what?

Constable 1: Reconcile you with the king! You are not cooperating at all!

Ebili *[rising]*: What do you need from me, really? I am no big name in this land. Your snuff is in your own hands, you and your king!

Constable 1: All right, it's down to us here. . . . . Let's talk about that broom.

Ebili: Talk does not stop a broom from sweeping!

Constable 1: Let's settle this like friends. We are only strangers in your place

Constable 2: Tell us as your own brothers, the answer to the broom . . .

Ebili *[diverts himself, whistling awhile]*: It is a deep and priceless kingdom secret.

Constable 1 *[intently]*: Our friendship is priceless as well. You will have our protection, easy passage . . . . many other privileges!

Constable 3:	Above all, nobody will ever harass you again in this land.
Ebili:	What about the pain you caused me already? Before now, you were all swaggering like you descended from the sky. Why should I save you from the pepper of the gods?
Constable 2:	Are we not fellow black skins? What will our death profit you?
Ebili:	I have no wish for your death but no joy in your life either. You wear that hateful cloth for the white man, and . . . *[He shrugs]*
Constable 1:	And what?
Ebili:	You are harsher than your white master. You carry death in your hands for him and from the look of things, you can't wait to destroy the birthplace of your own father.
Constable 3 *[indignantly]:*	That is an insult to our uniform.
Constable 1 *[restraining his colleague]:*	But I think he is right . . . . . in a way.
Constable 3 *[bristling]:*	We shouldn't accept an insult in any way!
Constable 1:	Let's be sincere for once, ourselves. Are there not moments when each of us has asked himself if there is something sewn into this cloth? This uniform of cloth and cap that we wear for the white man . . . . is there something in it that kicks us in the brains so we must do bold and senseless things from time to time? It worries me a lot whenever I think about it.
Constable 3:	Then stop thinking. That's the only right way to do this job!
Constable 1:	I'd love to stop thinking. It weighs me down too much. Like now, I'm feeling guilty that I slapped this man a moment ago. Why did I do it and why am I sad now? What's the sense?

Ebili:	Is that an apology to a power you have challenged by slapping a son of the soil in the very temple of his ancestors? Apology should never dance with a mask like a masquerade. If it truly wishes to find acceptance in a man's heart, why can't it come open-faced like a damsel that is sure of herself?
Constable 1:	You are right, brother. In short . . . . direct apology . . . . I am sorry.
Ebili:	And what about both of you?
Constables 2 & 3:	We too are sorry.
Ebili:	The palace of Umudimkpa has heard us all as brothers now.
Constable 1:	We have become brothers and friends. That is it!
Constable 2 *[shaking hands all around]:*	A brother in another land, the best gift of the gods!
Ebili:	It shouldn't be just handshakes; but alas, my wine pot is broken, the wine wasted! What can we drink together now as brothers? What can we share as children of same womb and sucklings of same breasts to seal this wonderful bond?
Constable 1:	That broom is the perfect bond, my brother. Share its magic with us, it will hold us together like a secret cult. All the power of a secret cult, what is it but a secret shared or a deadly deed covered for life by joint consent?
Ebili:	I see deep inside your heart; you truly want to know the truth.
Constables 2 & 3:	Everything about that broom. Everything!
Constable 1:	How to remove the curses from us; most urgent!

Ebili: Stand together then, all three of you . . . Face me . . . yes, face the East for sunrise, right . . . . this way, yes.

          [Shuffling, they stand beside one another and face him]

Ebili: Take a deep breath, now . . . . Deeper . . . . *[All breathe deep, deeper]*

Ebili: You see that broom? *[All nod expectantly]* No please! It is death to see that broom . . . . . The only way to survive it is . . . .

All *[anxiously]*:   Is what? Is what?

Ebili: Deny. Just that! Deny you ever saw the broom. Understand?

          [They nod glumly] No matter what anybody says to you, that broom is not there. Do you hear me? *[They nod, all eyes fixed on Ebili]* It does not exist; do you understand? *[All nod in rapt attention]* Don't say you were not warned . . . Any questions? *[All shake their heads]* Whoever sees a broom sees his own fever. For me, I see no broom; but that's me.

Constable 1:   I see no broom.

Constable 2:   Broom? Which broom? Where is it?

Constable 3:   Is there a broom? I see nothing.

Ebili: All right, friends. I must gather the remains of my princess now. She deserves a final resting place on the palace grounds.

Constable 1:   Sorry for all the pain we caused you.

Ebili: All is forgiven, my brother. You may join me at her graveside and pay your last respects . . .

          [Fade]

Act 1, Scene 4

Throne Room at Umudimkpa palace. A loud voice off-stage announces the king. Constables 2 & 3 enter and quickly inspect the throne room, then stand at attention at the entrance. Enter King Abednego followed by Sergeant.

Abednego: This is not a good way to start. Why is D.O. overturning all my plans? Suddenly, everything is upside down.

Sergeant: You are still king, O king.

> *[Abednego paces awhile, then waves off the two constables]*

Abednego: He should allow me do this job like a true king. Why interfere?

Sergeant: Interference is not good, my king!

Abednego: He says negotiate! That is weakness. What kind of king negotiates with conquered subjects? This is very, very annoying. Not what I expected at all.

Sergeant: But it may be a clever game he wants you to play, O king. You know how the white man behaves.

Abednego: How does he behave?

Sergeant: Like a lion that dresses like sheep and acts like a lamb, just to enter amongst sheep.

Abednego: I can play that game better than any white man. And I know my people best.

Sergeant: You know your people very well, O King.

Abednego:	The only peace my people respect is terror.
Sergeant:	I agree with you, king.
Abednego:	Nobody can rule my people without a strong fist to break their stubborn heads. That is why I ordered those big arrests.
Sergeant:	Big arrest is how you show them your power! When people see chiefs arrested, they sit down where you tell them to sit; they fear and obey without long talk. That is *gorment*, king.
Abednego:	Now, he's telling me to go and release the high chiefs.
Sergeant:	I am very worried, King. I am very, very worried about that.
Abednego:	He says we should detain only the young men and their leader, Egbuna who killed the white missionary.
Sergeant:	I see trouble in letting the high chiefs go, O king.
Abednego:	So what are you going to do about it?
Sergeant:	Shon sir! Anything you want me to do sir!
Abednego:	Listen Sergeant, you won't release anybody at all tonight.
Sergeant:	Shon sir! Let them suffer for one night at least.
Abednego:	Yes! By morning when we meet with them, they will be the ones dying to agree with us.
Sergeant:	Shon sir!
Abednego:	Go now and make sure that nobody gives them food or water.
Sergeant:	No food, no water?
Abednego:	Yes. That's what is called superior tactics!
Sergeant:	Shon sir! King sir.

Abednego:	And, no mats for anybody! They must sleep on the bare floor.
Sergeant:	There is even no space to lie down. We made it very tight like an animal cage and we pushed all of them in there, even the old woman.
Abednego:	That's wonderful, very good that they stand all night. Superior tactics! You are beginning to think in the head, Sergeant!
Sergeant:	Shon, O king! Superior tactics, sir!

[Exit Sergeant]

Abednego *[aside]*: A ruler must be strong or his subjects will ride on his head . . . . *[Rises and paces slowly]* One little sign of weakness, you become a sorry byline for silly tales by moonlight . . . . My problem is the high fools they call high chiefs. I must put them under my feet as subjects no matter rank or title! I have to use my own methods since my white friend has lost his bearing and now behaves like chicken in the rain. Umudimkpa must begin to fear the mention of my name. What else is power?

[Voices within, in a shouting match]

Ugochi's voice:	How dare you? Come on, clear out of my way!
Lance Corporal's voice:	Woman, go back! You cannot enter.
Ugochi's voice:	May the coconut of wicked spirits break your foolish head. Do you know me?
Lance Corporal's voice:	Who are you? Are you not a woman again?
Ugochi's voice:	Get out of my way or spirit pepper will blind your staring eyes!
Lance Corporal's voice:	You cannot enter unless the king calls for you.
Ugochi's voice:	It is the mad wind of these evil times! Slime and scum are blown into palaces; a common dog stands to argue with me eyeball to eyeball! Go

in there, you nameless clown, and tell Apiti that the daughter of a real king is here to see him now.

Lance Corporal's voice: The daughter of which king? Who are you calling Apiti?

[Abednego cocks his ear, listening to the exchange]

Ugochi: Don't stand there talking back at me, you hireling from the roadside of lunatics. Go and tell your master that Ugochi, Princess of Umuachala and wife of Orimili Umudimkpa is here for him. I will dash in there and scratch out his eyes if you keep me waiting a moment longer.

Abednego *[shouting]*: All right, Corp'l! If she is alone, the princess is welcome in my royal presence! Bring her in!

[Enter Ugochi, Lance Corporal following at a respectful distance. Abednego is grinning, one foot up the dais. Ugochi unimpressed, hisses disdainfully.]

Abednego *[to Lance Corporal]*: Leave us alone . . . . And let nobody interrupt!

Lance Corporal: Shon sir! King, sir!

[Exit Lance Corporal]

Abednego: The years stood still, great princess. A glimpse of you still pulls the strings of melody in a man's heart.

Ugochi: Your brand of madness is without remedy; but though it took a whole century, it is about to kill you.

Abednego: I am king, now, Ugochi. I command the stars in the sky to bow for this moment of reunion. You are the blaze of beauty still.

Ugochi:	You are still Apiti, the evil mud. I hear you've taken a new name. How many names will change the pig in a pig?
Abednego:	Flog me with cusswords. Just go on, sweetheart. I have missed this for twenty years.
Ugochi:	You are still a scoundrel, a pig and nothing better!
Abednego:	Thanks, precious, thanks. I recognize the crude barbs of pure original love. Wound me with them till I die dreaming of you.
Ugochi:	You disgust me, same today as years ago. Nothing is sacred in your accursed eyes; no honey is sweet enough except the forbidden one. Shame (*tufiaa!*) to any woman you deceive with your pretences.
Abednego:	Pretences? Is that what you think of my avowed love? Can you ever guess my pain of years, seeing you go off with half-men, empty bearers of bloated titles who never deserved a bit of you? First it was that tragic fool, Ifediba, insulting your pride as a woman . . .
Ugochi:	You are the one that misled him; you manipulated the idiot because he was basket-brained enough to trust you.
Abednego:	Every monkey that plays with his age mates should be smart enough to mind the length of his own tail. That's my view of life and it is working very well for me. Ifediba was stupid.
Ugochi:	Yes, he was stupid because he trusted you. He had no idea what you are!
Abednego:	What am I? Say it to my face. Say it and let me hear.
Ugochi:	Is it still a secret to anyone? You are an unconscionable snake, for ever sneaking behind your betters to rob them of their best treasures.

Abednego *[roars with laughter]*: Who are my betters? The fool that killed himself rather than marry you or the one that married you rather than kill himself?

Ugochi: The gods will stuff your mouth with your entrails if you dare abuse my husband.

Abednego *[with mocking laughter]:* Husband! Husband! Husband! You sound like those cocoyam housewives who love to pretend to the whole world that their marriage is the sweetest banquet on earth. Do you think I haven't heard about your frequent quarrels with Obiora?

Ugochi: And what is your business what I do with my husband?

Abednego: Ah! Anything about you is my business, Ugochi. Besides, I am king and will not tolerate domestic violence in my kingdom. It won't be business as usual going forward. There must be peace in every home.

Ugochi: Apiti, I am here to take my husband home. Release him now or Amadiora will strike you down like the dung heap you are.

Abednego: I know you are in love with me. It's just that the woman in you makes you deny, like it will kill you to admit it.

Ugochi: Apiti, you are the faeces of a demented pig! May maggots from the evil forest eat out your rotten eyeballs!

Abednego: Ah, ah! Don't forget you are a born princess. And don't forget I am king. Language must be clean in my royal presence.

Ugochi: Royal has become a password for mumps and maggots! Release my husband, Apiti! Release my husband, now!

Abednego:	Which husband are we even talking of? Is it not that baby face called Obiora? He will rot in the pit in case you don't know.
Ugochi:	If that was your plan, you forgot there is me to contend with.
Abednego:	What are you going to do? Skin my head?
Ugochi:	I've been to that camp that you think nobody else but you can muster legs to enter. I have seen your white master face to face.
Abednego:	You went to see D.O.?
Ugochi:	He is a mortal like us and I told him things he will never forget.
Abednego *[aside]*:	Fools everywhere! Fools around me! *[Turns to Ugochi]* Ugochi, who permitted you to see D.O.?
Ugochi:	A world that needs your permission to breathe is a graveyard. A creature like you can never be in control of my movement or destination!
Abednego:	Of course, you now prefer a white skin. I can feel something in your trembling voice and glistening eyes. It's like the first whiff of a powerful drink, isn't it? Goes *bam!* like this, straight to the brains, arrests the senses and puts you in a momentary jail of ecstasy.
Ugochi *[sneering]*:	What is he talking about?
Abednego:	What are you doing with the white man? Trust me, tell me. I won't tell your husband . . .
Ugochi:	What do you mean?
Abednego:	I'm the one asking. What are you doing with him? Do you know anything of him? Do you even hear his language?
Ugochi:	Thank heavens; Apiti is no longer the only interpreter in this land.

Abednego:	That fool, Hezekiah! Can he interpret his toes from his fingers? You only heard what he pretended to you.
Ugochi:	I heard right and I can't be confused by you, Apiti. The man you call Dio has told me in very clear terms that he ordered you to release my husband. I am here to see that you do it without your usual tricks. Release my husband or I go back and report you to the man you take as your god!
Abednego:	Ugochi . . . . Ugochi, why are you talking like this to me? Jokes apart . . . really, every joke apart, did I ever say your husband won't be released? I think I deserve a gesture of appreciation from you for my acts of kindness to you. A hug or something better may be a good start.

[Tries to hug her but she shoves him off angrily]

Ugochi:	How dare you? Dio must hear this first thing tomorrow!
Abednego:	Hear what?
Ugochi:	That you even demanded a sexual hug in payment or you won't release my husband.
Abednego:	Husband, husband! Hear what you hate to face, Ugochi. If not for my goodness to you, it is the corpse of that silly boy that would be begging for disposal now!
Ugochi:	You may be prince of parrots; but I'm never tickled by your fang-is-finger stories.
Abednego:	That is not a nice thing to say to the paramount ruler of all Umudimkpa!
Ugochi *[snorting]*:	Paramount ruler! You, Apiti!
Abednego:	Yes, that's me, the *Ogbu onye ubosi ndu n'aso ya*, the One who kills a person on the sweetest day of his life!

[Ugochi emits a long-drawn hiss of contempt]

Abednego:	I am still the man you should be thankful to.
Ugochi:	Thank you ever for what, Apiti?
Abednego:	First for your own life . . . and for your own freedom! And most of all, for my royal decision to spare that spoilt child you call husband. Was it not only a moment ago, just before you came in here, that I summoned the headman of the police and gave him orders? I told him to go at once and set Obiora free! What again do you want from me?
Ugochi:	Only one thing, Apiti. Leave me and my husband out of your countless plots and tricks. Otherwise all the vultures in this world will camp on your rotten head!
Abednego:	I really don't know how else to please you, Ugochi. I am the one who worried and wearied Dio for the release of Obiora, all for your sake. But what am I getting in return? You now adore a white skin, somebody whose mouth is saying "come" when his heart is saying "go".

[Re-enter Sergeant]

Sergeant:	Shon, sir, King sir! All correct! Detainees will be there till dawn, by your last order. No food, no water, no mat to lie down!
Abednego:	Are you out of your mind, Sergeant? Which detainees, whose order? You wicked man! Why punish innocent people?
Sergeant:	Ah! King! But you ordered me to . . . .
Abednego:	Shut up your mouth! You are so dense, the only listening hole in your body is your anus!
Sergeant *[chastised and confused]:*	All correct, sir! No complain', king!
Abenego:	Now, hear it well from me. Have you no respect? The woman standing here, do you know who

she is? A true princess is who she is! I told you a dozen times to release her husband. I am just hearing from her that you didn't do it. Is it that you don't know which one is called Orimili Obiora? Why do you take forever to carry out a simple instruction? Release him at once!

Ugochi: Not only Orimili Obiora! Dio called the other names too—Oyidia, Akaeze, Oche-ilo-eze—every one of them!

Abednego: We are saying the same thing. Must a king repeat himself?

Ugochi: Let him hear all the names at once because I am going with him right up to that door. All must come out together and all must be in sound health or your eyes will see blood in your drinking cup! You, there, fat man, you've heard everything. Follow me straightaway!

[Exit Ugochi]

Abednego *[To Sergeant, aloud]*: What are you still waiting for? Go and release the good people!

Sergeant: Shon, sir! King! *[Heads to the door]*

Abednego *[voice lowered]*: Come back here, Sergeant. Where are you going?

Sergeant *[confused]*: You said I should go and release . . . .

Abednego: Go and release who? Sergeant, are you a fool?

Sergeant: King sir, but you told me just now to . . . .

Abednego: I told you nothing. Think in the head. Nobody goes till daybreak!

Sergeant: Shon sir! But what shall I tell the waiting princess?

Abednego: Arrest her as well!

Sergeant: King sir, that could be big trouble if D.O. hears.

Abednego:	Think in the head, Sergeant. We arrested her to save her life. There were assassins, did you forget?
Sergeant:	Shon sir, King! Yes, the assassins. They were plotting to kill her this very night but the information was leaked to us, so we took her in to protect her. It was done in her own best interest.
Abednego:	Brilliant, Sergeant! Brilliant! Protective custody. Find room for her quickly!
Sergeant:	Shon sir, King!

[Exit Sergeant]

Abednego *[Aside]*:	I will never be a costume-and-foofoo king if that is what you people are expecting. I'm nobody's loin cloth! Umudimkpa must feel my full weight! They must know which one of two turtles is the true male!

[He puffs on his pipe. Enter Constables 3 and 2]

Constable 3:	Oga Abadi!
Abednego *[flares up]*:	Don't you ever call me that nonsense again! Are you mad?
Constable 3:	Sorry, king sir! King!
Abednego:	What nonsense! Because I allow you into my royal presence? Oga Abadi, he says in my face . . . like I'm just an individual!
Constable 2:	We are sorry sir, king sir.
Abednego:	Dare me with a repeat! Baby dog does not know the limit of a mere cuddle! Contempt is the abusive child of familiarity!
Constable 3:	It won't happen again sir, king sir. We are very sorry, king.
Constable 2:	Forgive our mistake, king. Your boys are sorry.

Constable 3:	Happy to report that we have arrested the one called Ebili.
Abednego:	I'm no longer in the mood to see that fool anymore. Turn him loose!
Constable 2:	Oga Aba—sorry, King, you told us to . . . .
Abednego *[shouting]:*	Get away from here! Have you people gone fully mad? I said release him. Release! Free the man! Free him and let me breathe! Why are you staring like that at me?

[Perplexed, both constables head to the door]

Constables 2 and 3:	All right, sir . . . . All right king, sir.
Abednego:	Get back here both of you! Didn't you see that broom?
Constable 2:	Broom?
Constable 3:	Which broom, king?
Abednego:	Are you blind in the eye? Each one of you has been stepping around that thing and you ask me which broom! Can't you simply pick it up and keep it in a proper place?
Constable 2:	I . . . . don't see any broom, king.
Constable 3:	There is no broom, king.
Constable 2:	If there was a broom, I'd be the first to put it away, O king.
Abednego:	What is wrong with both of you? Are you telling me you can't see with your eyes?
Constable 2:	King, but there is no broom where you are pointing.
Constable 3:	Nothing is there at all.
Abednego:	All right, hold on, just hold on! *[Raises his voice]* Who is there at the door? Come in quickly. Come in now, now, now!

[Enter Constable 1 and Ebili]

Constable 1:	Long live the king!
Abednego:	Correct greeting! Correct greeting. You seem the only one with sense amongst these empty heads.
Constable 1:	Thank you, king. Long live the king.
Abednego:	Tell me straightaway what you see there on the floor.
Constable 1:	Where O king?
Abednego:	There, where my finger is pointing! What is wrong with you too?
Constable 1:	I see nothing, king.
Abednego:	You see nothing?
Constable 1:	Nothing is there. Is anyone saying there is something?
Constable 2:	We asked that same question.
Abednego:	Shut up all of you! I am the one asking questions here!
Ebili *[whistles a carefree tune and chuckles]*:	Those who plan to sell heads in the market should first secure a hiding place for their own . . .
Abednego:	You too, shut up your mouth! Did I ask you to speak?
Ebili:	I didn't speak to you the rumble in your ears . . . . The rousing of our forefathers . . . . A fake dance now a shambles On the slippery path!
Abednego:	You are a shame of wasted years. But your sorrows are totally private. The echoes of battle in a drunkard's ears belong to his head alone. Shut your mouth in my presence except I ask you to speak!

Ebili [*chuckling again*]:   Ambush of thorns, a gift of loose baskets
                                  Gathering home a harvest of broken bones

Abednego [*to Ebili*]:   I won't tolerate another provoking word from you! What do you even want here by the way?

Ebili: Ah, if the wind is wondering what it picked up,
Boon to my ears,
The more the laughter rumbling
In the sacred groves.

Abednego: Power is mine. I ordered you to come and I can order you to go. I am king over you. I can deal with you. So now, out! Go! Leave my palace!

Ebili: Away, like a sunbird merrily . . . what's my own? The caprices of empty wind cannot offend my peace.

Abednego: Get lost. I don't need your drunken breath around here for now! I will take my time, make up my mind about you and your sort, what to do with you. The kindness of time has delivered you all into my hands.

Ebili: The kindness of years should remind you that fear fears Ebili.

Apiti: Get out of my palace.

Ebili: You must hear this first, Apiti, by whatever name you confuse the world for now. Nightfall has its own designs for the clever creep. Beware things you see that no one else can see and things everyone can see but you alone cannot see.

Abednego: Get out of here, stupid! Get out!

Ebili: Merrily like a sunbird . . . . Still beware; the palace of the king is not a refuse dump. The fatal laughter of our forefathers follows all reckless feet.

Abednego [*to his constables*]:   Get this drunkard out of here!

Ebili:	Stop trying to push these poor strangers into errors. They have a right to live and not die like you.

[The constables shift uncertainly. Ebili turns at the door]

Abednego *[hissing derisively]*: Empty sounds of an empty barrel!

Ebili: You will find no sleep in the echoes of night, the words of my mouth watching you like daggers from the rafters.

Abednego: Hear this much of my royal intention before you leave—just a little intimation of my thoughts for a small fry that I could squash right now. That I chose to keep you floating for just a few more days is because there is this little entertainment value in you that might be useful at my coming coronation. You will perform to please my guests and make them laugh. That is your last chance to impress me as a fool forever! Keep that in mind, drunkard.

Ebili: Without doubt, this kingdom permits every dreamer a fancy name for himself! A rat has every right to call himself a leopard and live out his own conceits. But the eyes of the ages have been streaming with tears for only one idiot. The pretender so badly cursed by his maker and so confused or consumed by his own madness that he lays a finger on the throne of Umudimkpa! Apiti, I dare you to your face: be the first to dare!

Abednego: Your spite and jealousy can do nothing to me! I am king of all Umudimkpa. Paramount ruler, that's me! Even the white man is working for me. I will sit on the throne of my fathers!

Ebili: Throne of whose fathers? Did I hear you well?

Abednego: What can a cockroach hear in the heat of vapours?

Ebili: That throne is your waiting test of manhood . . . . The fabled laughter of our forefathers has found a live object . . . A deaf man knows the outbreak of war without hearing a sound.

                 [Exit Ebili, the constables following. Abednego paces in the dimming light . . . . Fade]

ACT 1, SCENE 5

Throne Room at Umudimkpa palace. In the half light of pre-dawn, the broom on the floor is encircled with a bold white chalk mark. Ojongo, the juju priest is beating his small rusty gong and skipping around the broom on one leg, his face and bare torso tattooed with white chalk. His mat is spread out in one corner and piled with knick knacks from his emptied goat-skin bag.

Ojongo: Ojongo has neither friends nor enemies! Ojongo never asks the cause of a fight or the purpose of a feast. Where he is called, Ojongo will come. What he owes the spirits, a fair share of the spoils! Choi! Choi! Choi!! Ojongo is standing on one leg, the uncertainty of a newcomer cock in a vast compound. Speak to me, ancient furies that guard the portals of wisdom. Name what you eat that I may feed it you and pass by with wholesome feet!

                [He hops to his mat and squats on it, hangs a thickly beaded necklace around his neck and casts pebbles]

Ojongo: Ojongo, hear yourself, Deity that nurses the baby lion for the lioness! There is no mountain that feet cannot climb. But whose feet? Choi! Choi! Choi! Behold . . . darkness is fading; time for quickened steps, the shy ones to round off their secret dance or face exposure by the coming light of dawn. Many would shun Ojongo in the daylight but by night, they come naked. It is the way of the world to pretend to the world. Ojongo holds his place by powers that push him

and forces that pull him. Choi! ChoiChoi! We
are here together, the visible and the invisible;
we mingle to raise up or raze down. If this
night's summon is blood, here is a white cock!
[He lifts a flapping cock] If a clash of heads, the
curved horns of a tethered ram lie in wait in the
back yard. Here is kola, here is snuff and here
your portion of hot drink. Eat your share now
and lend your strength of battle to the suppliant
warrior. Ojongo makes enquiry and presumes
nothing . . .

> *[He pours libation, takes a gulp and rinses his mouth, then blows a noisy spray upward. He shakes his rattles and hums a tune]*

Ojongo:

The arena is stripped for a dance of the spirits.
Is there a pot that can empty a river? What
Ojongo has not invoked must not convoke. The
dawn that kills both sojourner and host adds
a foul stench to an ugly tale. Ojongo is set for
any question. The questioners may now come
forward. *[He beats his gong thrice and resumes shaking the rattles]*

Ojongo *[shouts]:*

Come forward, Strong Heads that called Ojongo
out of sleep! Come and hear the wisdom that
kills those that won't find it.

> *[Enter King Abednego followed by the three constables]*

Abednego:

Speak full into my ears. It cost me a fortune to
bring you here.

Ojongo:

Only the living count cost.

Abednego:

What of the dead?

Ojongo:

They are the final cost in themselves. The mighty
gods who spared you against odds must not be
angered by cost counting. The fortune that is
saved by a miserly fool is like a noontime bat

that can only fly blind. For whom does it perch in the end? It is for mockers and strangers . . . . and even enemies!

Abednego: I am no fool. I know I have plenty of mockers and enemies.

Ojongo: They are many more than you can imagine! Some are plotting your downfall, some your painful death. Some have sworn that the food you eat will turn to stones in your stomach . . . . But Ojongo is sitting here and watching all that are watching you. Ojongo knows what to do if he is asked to do something.

[Abednego squats facing Ojongo on the mat. The constables stand at a nervous distance in the corner]

Abednego: Tell me first about that broom. I want to know who sent it.

[Ojongo laughs mirthlessly. He plays his rattles intermittently]

Ojongo: Am I to believe that you don't even know your own enemies?

Abednego: My question is why do I see a broom that my bodyguards, the people I trust with my life, cannot see?

Ojongo *[with an impish chuckle]:* Are you still a stranger to the wickedness of men and their offspring? Your enemies are powerful and they will stop at nothing! They have sent you *okpokikpo,* the broom of incurable madness to drive you from the palace. But Ojongo knows what to do if he is asked to do something.

Abednego: First, you will remove that broom immediately.

Ojongo: That is not a problem, but there's a whole lot more to do for you. Cobwebs do not trap a spider. Floods cannot drown a fish, and the countenance of the forest cannot stop a wild monkey from a good jump on the trees.

Abednego: How much is the cost?

Ojongo: Shackles may play their vicious part; but freedom is the destiny of baboon. This work will eat something from your hands.

Abednego: Name your price.

Ojongo: It is four she-goats, two bags of money and a cow with fighting horns.

Abednego: I shan't contest your demand. But it shall be judgment if you fail me. Begin immediately. You will be paid at dawn. *[Rises from the mat]*

Ojongo: Ojongo takes his full pay in advance or he works for no mortal.

Abednego: How can you expect delivery of cow and goats at this time? Look at the time of night.

Ojongo: Deliver the livestock to my house at dawn. For now, you will bring me the two bags of money; then I will disable that broom for a start.

Abednego: You must remove it completely.

Ojongo: Ojongo knows what to do.

Abednego *[snaps his fingers at his constables]*: Get him the money.

[Constables 2 & 3 exit and return with two bags of cowries. They lay them before Ojongo on the mat. He opens the bags and checks, then ties them back with a satisfied nod and rises.]

Ojongo: Ojongo is up on two legs, like a rearing ram. Money is the sharpness of a matchet, riches the strength of a man's heart. Even if spirit crowds converge with bragging drums against this day, Ojongo has been asked to do something.

[He gathers his stuff into his goatskin bag and rolls up his mat]

Ojongo *[to Abednego, indicating the constables]:* What is your real plan for these three men? Tell me your heart.

Abednego: They are my trusted agents who would do secret things in my name. Anything to put fear in my subjects!

Ojongo: You have chosen well. And these ones will do it well if the right thing is done for you. Ojongo knows what to do if he is asked to do something.

Abednego: Finish with the broom first. That's the trouble of now.

Ojongo: Of course, the broom first. The broom of evil must go first.

[Ojongo takes out a white cloth from his goatskin bag and stepping backwards, drops it over the broom on the floor. He blows chalk powder to the four corners.]

Ojongo: The strong eye has sighted what the thickest fog had covered. Rabbit has shut his mouth; Squirrel would not utter a word. Only the swamp toad is set tonight to tell a tale of the marshlands . . . . Whirlwinds, take your share of kola nut; pepper shrub, have your own share. The weapon made to kill an elder is deadliest when it is fashioned as a child's plaything.

[He puts a palm-frond bit between his jaws, stuffs the two bags of money into his big goatskin bag and clamps the rolled mat under his left arm. He slings the goatskin bag over his right shoulder and humming a mystery tune, steps backwards to the covered broom. He stoops and without looking back, picks up the cloth and broom with his left hand. Exit Ojongo.]

Constable 3 *[conspiratorially]:*   King sir, are we to follow and recover the money?

Abednego: Leave that to me. Everything will come back.

Constable 3:   His demands are too much.

Abednego: No matter. We need him on our side for now.

Constable 2:   But people hate him too much, O king.

Abednego: People are stupid, which is why they must have a ruler like me.

Constable 2:   We can find you a medicine man with a better reputation. This one is hated everywhere.

Abednego: Dreaded you mean, which is what suits me perfectly at this very moment. I need powerful charms to subdue the whole kingdom and rule this people like nobody would make *fim.*

Constable 1:   Your wisdom is great, O king.

Constable 3:   It is wisdom from the gods!

Abednego: But you three have become my only worry. You are no better than spirit infants! How can I trust you as bodyguards? That simple broom would have killed you off like baby insects!

Constable 2:   Forgive, O king. Your enemies will be like ash always and a mere snort of your nostrils will blow them off to never return.

Constable 3:   Those who hate you will never find laughter. We shall spare nothing to crush them all for you.

Abednego: With empty words? Where is your strength?

Constable 3:   Great One, we shall find strength very quickly. Better to die than to fail you. We shall destroy anybody who opposes you!

Abednego: Stop! My ears burn when grown-up men stand before me and blab like infants. Are mountains

	climbed with mere wishes or battles won with empty words?
Constable 3:	Great One, it is not empty words. We are ready to die for you!
Abednego:	What use are three dead bodies to me? I need men alive who can think in the head, men who don't imagine that they could climb the mighty iroko with bare hands!
Constable 2:	We are your loyal bodyguards, Great One. We will never give you cause to question our loyalty, O King.
Abednego:	The cobra has no reason to fear betrayal. The hopping frog behind his back is still within a striking distance of his spit. I can wear all three of you around my waist like live amulets! You can never turn against me . . . . otherwise, the deadly oath you drank would finish you for me. I can sleep with both eyes closed because the oath I fed you is forever, no matter what you wish. No power on this earth can change it now.
Constable 3:	We have no wish to change it, Great One. It is a privilege to work for you. We are sworn to be loyal for ever.
Abednego:	What is loyalty without ability? It is disgusting . . . . like a crippled beggar that you want to kick in the face as he comes with fawning prostrations, crawling up your doorsteps . . . . .
Constable 2:	Ah!!
Abednego:	Why is this one saying ah? Enemies sent a deadly broom here to attack me; did anyone of you have the eyes to see it? If your king wasn't *Okponku Ga Agaa n'Ogwu*, the Tough Cookie that Survives Thorns and Brambles, where is your own story?

[Constables all kneel in supplication]

Constable 1:	Forgive us, Great One; it is a war of the mightiest spirits!
Constable 3:	What we need is power to see like wild cats. We shall fight like mad dogs and your enemies are dead in the shadows!
Abednego:	Ojongo is coming back. He will cook you like old-time warriors.
All Constables *[prostrating fully]:*	Thank you, Great One. Thank you.
Abednego:	I take no thanks of empty words.
Constable 3 *[half rising]:*	Not empty words, Great One. This is the pledge of our lives. We shall serve you like a god.
Abednego:	Lie down properly, all of you . . . . and listen to me very well.

[They lie prostrate before him. Lights dim.]

I am investing heavily in security because, as a rule, I never leave anything to chance. I shall feed the forbidden spirits of darkness whatever they love to eat so they back me on my throne. You will merely be their human bodies. I hope that is clear. *[He steps roughly over their still bodies]* This is no moonlight play. I am buying you three for life. Anyone of you who attempts to betray me shall die an orphan like a day-old chick. He will die with his household . . . . and I mean, Die!!

[Fade]

ACT 1, SCENE 6

King's Public Square at Umudimkpa. In the grey half light of early dawn, a knot of people forms slowly. Three women of various ages carrying empty water pots stand dejectedly in the corner.

1st Woman: What you hear on all roads is 'Go back! Go back!' Swine with evil guns are blocking every pathway. You cannot go to the stream! You cannot go to the farm! 'Go back! Go back!' Like the barking of mad dogs! You can't even see the faces and mouths shouting those grunts.

2nd Woman: We assemble here. When it is full daybreak, we shall go in the strength of numbers. Let's see who can stop us then.

3rd Woman: I am much worried about my husband. He was unwell last night but when they came to grab him, he escaped with his matchet to join his fellows in the bush.

1st Woman: My husband guessed they would come; he was gone before they came for him.

3rd Woman: Are they arresting men of every age?

1st Woman: My husband is young enough! What do you want to tell me? Even older men than him were taken away too!

3nd Woman: They said Gosiora and Osilike Age Grades only.

2nd Woman:	That's what they said but what we saw is different; they were picking up every adult male.
1st Woman:	Our men would show them that warriors are warriors. Tobacco snuff is no powder for the eye.
2nd Woman:	Our men will fight from the bush, but is that not the easier part? The real war is here with us at home and we the women are the ones to fight it.
1st woman:	You are right. The enemy has moved in to eat and sleep with us. Things will never be the same again.
3rd Woman:	That boy, Egbuna, he has really put us in a cooking pot. He should never have fired that shot.
2nd Woman:	What is done cannot be undone. A white man has been killed in Umudimkpa.
3rd Woman:	Is that why my head must carry a load I did not fetch?
1st Woman:	I have no problem if our brother took on a bad white man and killed him in the fight. But this person that was killed, everyone knows he was a gentle lamb. Look over there. That was his tent, his last place of abode in our land.
2nd Woman:	And that is his famous box. Out of that box, he was giving out free medication and other gifts. I was hoping to get a fine mirror for myself someday . . . That hope has died with him.
	[Blackout. Spotlight falls on Rev. Jones' box and tent, a doleful tune playing softly. Enter Iwobi, hobbling slowly on a staff. He halts, regards the box awhile, shakes his head ruefully, the spotlight brightening slowly on him]

3rd Woman:	Is that not Ogbuefi Iwobi, the great palm-wine tapper that was paralysed and bed-ridden for two years?
1st Woman:	Did you not hear? The white man healed him yesterday.
3rd Woman:	Too many unbelievable stories have been flying around lately. Didn't they say the white man called him a witch?
1st Woman:	Only the two of them know what manner of charms they were hurling at each other . . . . or why they camped out here day and night like ancient wizards all through the festival . . . .
3rd Woman:	But death has killed his white partner; what brings him again?
2nd Woman:	We better shift before our eyes see a forbidden thing.

[Exeunt the three women. Full black-out on stage as a macabre tune limbers up. Intermittently, deep guttural voices hum unintelligible chants that heighten a feeling of dread. Slowly the spotlight breaks on Iwobi, seated on the big box, head bowed, staff in hand, back leaned on the tree behind. He is dozing deep, his dream enacting itself on the stage, beginning with an eerie exchange off-stage between an elder's voice and his own . . . .]

Elder's voice:	Ogbuefi Iwobi, headman of the Ozuomee clan, what are you doing on a dead man's box?
Iwobi's voice:	This man's death is a personal loss to me, Great Elders. I feel devastated. The grief is killing me.
Elder's voice:	You have chosen to carry a strange load on your bare head? That man was not one of us.
Iwobi's voice:	He was a stranger, true, and the colour of his skin was not the colour of our own; still he should

not have died. I mourn him like my mother's son.

Elder's voice: Can sentiments stop the swinging doors of fate, Ogbuefi Iwobi? Life and death are only twin gates. Eternity is one compound, the same unending dream.

Iwobi's voice: It was not a dream. That man lived. Now, he is dead. It is great pain to me and my children. He is dead.

Elder's voice: You stopped dancing even in the thick of our strongest drumming. Why did that happen, Ogbuefi? We beat the drums harder, till our knuckles were bruised and aching. Still, you refused to join us in the dance of all age.

Iwobi's voice: You must put those drums away. I have no wish to dance again with you.

[Deep groans and heavy grunts and growls]

Elder's voice: You cannot turn your back on your fellow titled men. Ogbuefi Dunkwu is getting angry with you . . . . Ogbuefi Asimonye, ever short on patience is fuming already . . . . Your feather is bright in the hand of Ogbuefi Onyekwelu . . . Mark the clouds in the face of Ogbuefi Aganafu; he has never been kept waiting like this.

Chorus *[in blood-curdling grunts]:* Ne-eever! Ne-eever!

Elder's voice: Can you feel the pain in their grumbling? What if they decide to see you face to face . . . . ? Face to face . . .

Chorus *[in blood-curdling grunts]:* Face . . . to . . . face!
Face . . . to . . . face!
Face . . . to . . . face!
Face . . . to . . . face!

Elder's voice: They will come . . . . they will come . . . your response must be heard straight from your own lips . . . We must be sure that it is the mouth of Ogbuefi Iwobi that uttered such a strange thing.

Chorus *[in blood-curdling grunts]:*   Let . . . us . . . see . . . him!
Let . . . us . . . see . . . him!
Let . . . us . . . see . . . him!

[Clanging metallic sounds . . . then, a thumping drum beat . . . Light dims]

Chorus *[in blood-curdling grunts]:*   We . . . . are . . . coming!
We . . . are . . . . coming . . . .

[Five bare-footed, aged men in dirty white toga and single-feathered caps file in, slowly. All have drums in hand but only the last elder is beating his own, a dull monotone. Only he speaks as the others mime to the muted eerie tune playing off-stage.]

Elder: Ogbuefi Iwobi, you refuse our call, so we come uncalled. It is your dance, your feather is bright and waiting . . . We shall complete the circle . . . the circle . . . . the circle . . .

[They begin to sway and weave, to form a ring about Iwobi still dozing on the big wooden box.]

Elder: You are one of us, Ogbuefi. We shall complete the circle . . . then you must come with us!

[Ogbuefi Iwobi sways slowly, eyes closed, still dozing. There is a slow build-up of the funereal sounds, the tension increasing as Iwobi slowly rises, swaying on his feet. Enter Rev. Jones in his white soutane, open bible in hand and ringing a bell. The five elders quickly turn their backs and huddle in one corner.]

Rev. Jones:	Believe this or die in ignorance, God has sent His Son that you may have life and have it more abundantly.
Iwobi:	My friend, ah! My friend, I thought you were dead.
Elder:	All of us are dead. You are one of us, Ogbuefi.
Rev. Jones:	Hear this, my friend. There is a gift of eternal life by God. I am here to share the news with you.

> *[A puffing sound and a cloud of smoke in the corner and Ajofia materializes beside the huddled elders.]*

Ajofia:	It is forbidden! You will not spread it here!
Iwobi:	But you too are dead, Ajofia! All Umudimkpa heard of it.
Ajofia:	Even so, Ogbuefi Iwobi, but we shall not die alone. You must come with us. You belong to us . . .
Elder:	Yes, you belong . . . . and the twin gates are open. Life and Death.

> *[They all begin to beat their drums and Iwobi is swayed in their direction. He takes a few dance steps]*

Rev. Jones:	Friend, you are not bound to go with them. The living has a choice. Choose Life, my friend. Choose Life.

> *[Iwobi turns slowly to Rev. Jones]*

Iwobi:	But life and death are twin gates, Eternity the same compound
Rev. Jones:	That is an ancient lie from the pit of darkness!
Iwobi:	But it is the voice of our forefathers!

Rev. Jones:	Not your forefathers but spirits of deception. Hear the truth for the truth shall make you free.
Elder:	Hear the drums, Ogbuefi Iwobi. This is your dance. And your feather is bright and ready . . .

[Iwobi turns uncertainly, about to go with them, hesitates]

Iwobi:	Is that not my glory, a gift from my dead fathers? They have come from eternity. It is an honour.
Rev. Jones:	Be not deceived, my friend. Behold, the works of darkness shall be destroyed! The light of truth is shining on you!

[Full lights on stage. Ajofia and the huddled elders cover their faces, groaning and keening horribly]

Chorus *[in blood-curdling wails]:*

Kill the light!

Kill the light!

Kill the light!

Rev. Jones:	The light shines in darkness, but darkness comprehends it not.
Elder:	Not we alone, not we alone . . . Why make us die alone? Why?

Chorus *[in blood-curdling grunts]:*

Why-y-y?

Why-y-y-y?

Why-y-y-y-y?

[Cursing and groping blindly, exeunt the figures]

Iwobi:	Ah. Stranger, you have offended our fathers; you've broken their cover of darkness.
Rev. Jones:	Those are not your fathers. They are demons from the pit.

Iwobi:	Whatever name you call them, it is a forbidden thing to bring light when the ancients arise from the dead to speak with us! Your light has cut them off and perhaps, driven them out forever through the everlasting door.
Rev. Jones:	Eternity has no exit gate my friend, but all earthly gates are temporal and the light of God separates the realms. The dead that speak on earth are not your friends; and the living that listen to them are dead like them.
Iwobi:	But you too are dead. I saw you die, even followed with my sons to where they dumped your body. Your man, Hezeka was crying with the rest of us because you took a death not meant for you.
Rev. Jones:	There is a gift of life that I will share with you and your people. Come, sit beside me on my box and you will learn more of the truth of life. I feel in you a strong thirst for the truth.

[Iwobi sits uncertainly. Rev Jones draws closer].

Iwobi:	Am I dreaming this or I have left the world of men? We do not even know each other's language. How come we understand ourselves? It must be a dream . . . . Is it not a dream?
Rev. Jones:	Life is like a dream but only the living can live out dreams, and every dream is born of hopes and fears. Things are not what they seem in this land of the living; but the just shall live by faith in the God of all creation.

[Enter Ebili and the three constables in furious argument]

Ebili:	You have covered the land with fear! Tension all over the country!
Constable 3:	Your people are to blame. You killed a white man.

Iwobi:	Is it not you they are talking about?
Rev. Jones:	They cannot see you and me.
Iwobi:	How do you know that?
Rev. Jones:	Because you are the one dreaming us all. If you snap your fingers, something will happen.

[Iwobi snaps his fingers and the four men freeze]

Iwobi *[surprised]*:	Are they dead?
Rev. Jones:	No, just confused like the rest of the living. They fight and struggle, bicker and quarrel, wasting their lives, chasing after shadows and things of no value. Nobody thinks eternity which is the sum of life.

Iwobi *[rises and slowly inspects the frozen figures, Rev. Jones following closely]*: Well then, let's leave these ones to their own confusion. I want more of this sum of life you have brought to my ears.

[Exeunt Iwobi and Rev. Jones. Instantly the four men regain activation]

Constable 2:	How can you oppose your king and expect peace?
Ebili:	Which king? What peace? This nonsense must stop!
Constable 3:	Are you going to fight white man?
Ebili:	Is he a god that nobody can tell him he is wrong? How can anybody make Apiti king?
Constable 1:	Look, the coronation will be great, like something never seen in this land. What really do you people have against this man? Is it not just his past?
Constable 3:	I think it is wrong to condemn anybody for his yesterday. There's no real greatness without a dirty past.

Constable 2:	If we go digging up the past, we are no better than scavengers and the smell of death will never go away.
Constable 1:	I see the trees around us as an evidence of life that teaches us the wisdom of life. They look so lovely; but beneath the ground, where eyes cannot reach, their roots suck dirt to give them life. Is that not how beauty feeds on ugliness, the sweet present on some rotten past?
Constable 3:	You are putting it too nicely. The raw truth is that the leaves and fruits which we devour every day are only so good in our eyes and nice in our mouths because the rot and roots that feed the trees are covered from our view.
Ebili:	Why drag trees and roots into this talk? I know Apiti more than you can find him in seven lifetimes. That man is evil. His wicked past clings to him like a foul stench that can never be washed off. Our people will never forget his atrocities!
Constable 2:	Do you think there is a past that a man cannot wash clean for himself? I doubt it.
Constable 1:	Once you have enough money, you can buy yourself a new image any time. It's all about good wine. Get enough people drunk enough, white becomes black overnight.
Constable 2:	That is the funny side of public memory. When the wine is sweet, nobody remembers the tapper was a thief.
Constable 1:	Who minds the beginning of a running story or the past of the story teller? People swallow refreshed lies and vomit empty chants every day. Isn't that what they call public opinion?
Constable 2:	Everywhere you look, people are complaining about evil men but evil men are ruling everybody.

Constable 3:　　　　　Umudimkpa have got their own king! Let him reign!

[Re-enter Iwobi, followed by Rev. Jones]

Constable 1:　　　　　Ahh! Is that not the white man that was killed?

Iwobi *[worried, whispers quickly]:*　　　But you said they can't see us?

Rev. Jones *[quickly]:*　　　You forgot to snap your fingers!

[Iwobi snaps his fingers. All freeze including Rev Jones.]

Iwobi *[puzzled, touches Rev. Jones]:*　　　Even you, friend? Are you confused also?

[Rev. Jones recovers instantly, shakes his head, still dazed]

Rev. Jones:　　　　　I am human, just like you. But you are the one dreaming us all.

[Slowly they inspect the frozen men. Iwobi retakes his seat on the wooden box. Black-out on stage. A flute is playing softly, then there is a sudden burst of noises off-stage, the sounds of running feet and loud shouts. A cock crows in the distance]

Umeji and Obinna *[off-stage]:*　　　Fa-a-ther! Where are you, father? Where are you?

[Spotlight on Iwobi, seated on the box, still dozing, staff in hand, alone on stage in the widening spotlight. Enter Umeji and Obinna, panting from exertion]

Umeji:　　　　　Ah, there he is.

[Iwobi is still dozing, oblivious as his sons approach]

Obinna:　　　　　Father! Father!

[Iwobi mutters in sleep. Umeji shakes him by the shoulder and he snaps awake]

Iwobi:	What? The sky was like coming down upon the clouds where the tall palm trees—oh! Ah! Where are we? Where am I?
Umeji:	Father, please get up. Let's get you home.
Iwobi *[sighs]:*	It was all a dream then . . . ah, only a dream, you say?
Umeji:	We must hurry, father. There is a big problem. Let's get you home.
Obinna:	The white man's people are beating up everybody they see on the road.
Iwobi *[rubbing his eyes]:*	The white man's people? But where is my white friend?
Obinna:	Father, what's wrong again? You were there with us yesterday when Egbuna shot him dead. Please let's go home.
Iwobi *[struggling to clear his mind]:*	Egbuna shot my friend?
Obinna:	Father, please get up. The white man and his servants regard nobody as friend this morning.
Umeji:	Egbuna who fired the gun has escaped from their hands!
Iwobi *[shocked]:*	Egbuna escaped!

["Egbuna escaped! Egbuna escaped!" echoes from all sides, sudden panic. The ekwe sounds a frantic war chant]

[Fade]

Act 1, Scene 7

Throne Room at Umudimkpa palace, early dawn. Abednego highly agitated paces the dais, Sergeant kneeling before him, Constables 1 and 3 watching fretfully.

Abednego: That report is your death sentence. Your life for his own!

Sergeant *[tearfully]*:   King, there were four men guarding him, king sir. Four good men, sir!

Abednego: You will hang with those four. No waste of gun powder.

Sergeant: Look at it well, great king . . . Those men were the best for the job; they were carefully selected. But that boy is a juju man's son. Strongest juju is what he used.

Abednego: Juju did not save his father who was juju god himself. Did he not die like a roasted rabbit in his own fire? You allowed that dangerous boy to escape . . . you will die in his place!

Sergeant: Ah, juju power! The men were guarding the hut very well, just that the inside became empty and they didn't know. King sir, he removed the thatch and escaped through the roof.

Abednego: You aren't even ashamed of the rubbish in your mouth. After all your boast of Chief Elephant and concubines!

Sergeant:	King, you will see my new hand I swear. My men are moving like fire! Egbuna must be found or all his relatives are dead!

[Shouting and wailing off-stage and on-stage even within the. audience. Uniformed men bludgeon shrieking natives]

Abednego *[mocking]:*	So you now know the other use of pepper, Sergeant? What about court orders? What about white man's law?
Sergeant:	You are king, sir. If you give me a second chance, every word of your mouth is final. When you sigh once, I kill twice!
Abednego:	I have an old friend to do it better for me. He's in prison far away in Onicha but Dio will get him out of that place for me.

Sergeant *[rises and approaches Abednego]*: King sir, I am still your best man for this job. I promise you will see my hand in a new way. I have brought something quality which your eyes need to see first . . . . . . This one cannot escape! *[Quick to the door, shouts]* Bring her in! Bring her in!

[Enter Akweke, a rustic beauty of about fourteen, skimpily attired in scant native skirt and breast-piece; Lance Corporal follows, but Sergeant quickly waves him off. Her poise spiteful and airs aloof, Akweke disdains the constables' wild catcalls. Abednego surveys her with a lewd smile, rubbing his hands]

Abednego *[Aside]:*	Ah ya! When you think your eyes have seen everything, something fresh just drops from the sky (Ah ya!) then you see you've never seen anything. Is this one not a mermaid? Ah ya!
Sergeant:	Her name is Akweke.
Abednego:	Oh, Akw'eke! Fabulous name for a fabulous look!

[Sings in appreciation, surveying her from different angles]

Akweke olima, Akw'eke olima
> *(O purest gem, O rarest gem)*

Dooh olimaima, dooh olima
> *(A pining for my precious gem)*

Akweke olima, Akw'eke olima
> *(O purest gem, O rarest gem)*

Dooh olimaima, dooh olima
> *(A pining for my precious gem)*

Akw'eke m'debelu n'onwo n'ozurozi
> *(Precious gem that I'd so carefully stowed away is all but gone)*

Dooh olimaima dooh olima
> *(A pining for my precious gem)*

Akw'eke m'debelu n'onwo n'ozurozi
> *(Precious gem that I'd so carefully stowed away is all but gone)*

Dooh olimaima dooh olima
> *(A pining for my precious gem)*

Sergeant:	That is a beautiful song, O king.
Abednego:	A sweet song of my people that still brings me the joys and aches of infancy. *[Indicating Akweke]* Where is she from?
Sergeant:	King, this is the very heart beat of the wanted man, the maiden on whose head he paid a fat dowry.
Abednego:	Egbuna wanted to marry this one?
Sergeant:	All is settled, king. She was to join him this very week.
Abednego:	The boy has good eyes.
Sergeant:	But I have good ears, O king. As soon as Egbuna escaped, I moved sharp to grab her. The cobra knows how to wait by an empty hole, timing the runaway squirrel for home-sickness.

Abednego [*laughing out loud*]: Sarge, Sarge! You are not as daft as you look!

Sergeant: Thank you, my king, sir. I promised you will see my new hand!

Abednego: Your hand is good, Sergeant . . . This hand is very good . . . Leave Akweke with me . . . . For security reasons, I must interview her privately . . . . It is an urgent matter of state. Leave her with me!

[Enter Lance Corporal, breathless]

Lance Corporal: Shon, King! We brought them sir! The chief man and woman!

Sergeant: Which man and woman? Don't disturb the king!

Lance Corporal: Disturb? King said bring Akaeze, bring Oyidi'a quick like fire! King, they are here.

Abednego: When the king is busy with matters of state, people must wait!

Sergeant [*salutes vibrantly*]: Shon sir! Carry go! [*hushes Lance Corporal*] Think in the head!

[Blackout]

Act 2, Scene 1

Total black-out on a bare stage. Silhouetted figures are seen in various crouching, squatting and stooping positions, groaning and keening. A soft dirge plays in the stillness as the spotlight picks out Ebili rising to stand on his feet in the midst of the keening pack.

Ebili:
Grief has fallen upon the whole country . . . . Shhh! You all say, don't talk aloud, don't talk aloud. I ask you why. Why won't I talk? What happens if I talk?

Chorus:
You will die, Ebili. They will kill you.

Ebili:
Kill which of me? I am dead already . . . . Like you all, my people, I am dead. We all are dead . . . .

Chorus:
Nobody wants to die. We have no wish to die.

Ebili:
But we are all dead. We died that very moment when evil arose in our midst and we dispersed to our homes instead of standing together to confront it. We all, one by one and to the last man, shut our doors and shut our mouths. For fear of death, we fell silent, same as the dead . . . . Fear has killed us, my people, and death is only a burial.

Chorus *[sighing and keening]*:   It is the hand of fate. Just the hand of fate!

Ebili:
Fate is the excuse of the faithless. Pain is upon this land. It is marching from hut to hut, full of threats and big sticks, swear words and smoking guns.

Chorus:	Our great ancestors will arise. They will fight for us!
Ebili:	The dead never fight or what use is life? No, they bear no arms in battle. They never live our lives for us and cannot make our choices. They are no fighting troops but when we take a stand, they could be strength in battle. Our ancestors are dead and gone and only come alive in our acts of courage, for the dead never arise except the living do.
Chorus:	Who will save us then? Someone must do something!
Ebili:	When will you wake up from your dream of death? You are the one you are waiting for; no one else will live your life for you!
Chorus:	But they are killing us! They are killing everybody!

[The chorus breaks into a louder wailing as Sergeant bursts in with a thunderous roar, three constables at his heels. They tear into the people, swinging truncheons viciously and beating half a dozen or so to the ground]

Sergeant:	Silence everywhere! Silence or you die!
Ebili:	Silence is death and death is silence.
Sergeant:	Who born dog? Silence or I break your head!
Ebili:	What's the thrill in breaking bones if not the screams of pain?
Sergeant:	Your loud mouth is causing too much trouble in this land! Shut up or I swear, I will scatter your pumpkin head!

[He aims his truncheon at Ebili's head but Constable 1 is quick to grab his raised hand. All three constables close in on Sergeant and whisper

frantically into his ears. Sergeant slowly nods and calms down]

Ebili: Those who impose silence import a plague to waste their generations in the name of peace. A death sentence on free speech is the grim graveyard of murdered truth! Rob a child of everything but not his right to cry.

Sergeant: That long grammar is not for me. These people deserve death! They killed a white man! They killed a whole white man!

[He beats people crazy, the constables joining the frenzy]

Constables: You killed a white man! You killed a white man!

Ebili: Stop! Hear the truth. Spare the innocent who cannot find a voice to speak or cry. It is the white man's gun that killed the white man's brother! Yes?

People *[chorus]*: Yeees!

Sergeant: Shut up, you donkeys! Can a gun shoot by itself? That gun was fired by your kinsman. Where is the killer? Where is Egbuna?

[He lunges again at the people, beating them up. The constables follow his example.]

Constables: Where is Egbuna? Where is Egbuna?

Ebili: Stop! You are not asking the right questions. Which Egbuna are you looking for? Which Egbuna will you find in these people? Your reckless beating of innocent citizens has turned one runaway child into a faceless army that guns cannot defeat. When power goes fighting shadows, every shade in the land becomes a wounded lion.

Sergeant: Do you know the power of white man? Nonsense of opinion! Nonsense in private! You want to see

	the power of white man? You will see the power of white man! *[He attacks the people again, and the constables follow suit]*
Constables:	You will see the power of white man! You will see the power of white man! You will see . . .
Ebili:	Stop! White man himself has run back to Ubulu! Who has not heard that Ubulu went up in smoke last night?
Sergeant:	That is a small matter. Dio will put out that fire and come back here very quickly to bury his brother.
Constable 3:	He will bury his brother and install the king on the throne!
Ebili:	How many goats will be left in this land? How many sacks of meal and tubers of yam? Your men are stripping the barns, draining the vats . . . . carting away the substance of the people. What do you call that if not theft?
Sergeant:	Your people are not serious about tax! They must pay their taxes! Pay your taxes! *[Beats up on them, the constables following]*
Constables:	Pay your taxes! Pay your taxes! Pay your taxes! Pay . . .
Ebili:	Stop!
Sergeant:	Wrong! Tax cannot stop!
Ebili:	Tax? Are there still enough gunmen left to collect the taxes? Is anyone counting the number of dead bodies on both sides?
Sergeant:	More troops are coming! A lot more troops are already on their way to Umudimkpa! Your people cannot win this war. No, you cannot win!

Constables *[lashing out at the people]*:   You cannot win! You cannot win! You cannot win!

Ebili:	Stop! You too cannot win! Dozens of your troops are already sharing the hidden bush paths with frightened rabbits. Many have pulled off their fancy clothes and run back to their worried mothers. Umudimkpa is never late to battle!
Sergeant:	Forget that worthless boast. It is from a distant past that can never return. Your country is like a naked virgin right inside the bedroom of a manly king.
Ebili:	Beware your conclusions; beware the peepholes at the royal bedchambers. The eyes of death are peeping back at you!
Sergeant:	Death has no eyes. He is a blind killer . . . or why else are there law courts?
Ebili:	You seem to know him on first name terms like I never will. But beware his groping hands and the dark pit at your feet!
Sergeant:	A pit at my own feet? How do you mean?
Ebili:	There is something in that palace that eats pretenders. Yes?
People [chorus]:	Ye-e-e-es!
Sergeant:	Pretenders? Who do you call pretenders?
Ebili:	Small men who belittle their neighbours in a bid to look tall, guests who push people out of their own homes, strangers who regard the king's throne as a dumb chair. Pretenders, yes?
People [chorus]:	Ye-e-e-es!
Sergeant:	Nonsense of opinion! Nonsense in private! We shall see what is what! All the females, this side!
Women:	Why? For what?
Sergeant:	Because Egbuna is a man, and women must not suffer for the wrongs of men . . . . Besides, these ones are bush men!

Constables *[beating up on men]*:	Bush men! You are bush men! Bush men!
Ebili:	Stop beating about the bush! You're killing innocents!
Sergeant:	By the king's orders, we protect good women from reckless men. Women of Umudimkpa, yes?
Women:	Ye-e-s!
Sergeant:	Your suffering is over! It is your time for better life.
Women *[to themselves]*:	Better life is not bad. Everybody wants better life.
Sergeant:	Only for women! Beautiful ones will see the face of the king and the king will see beautiful faces too. By the order of the king, all the females, this side!
Constables:	This side! This side! *[About a half of the women move]*
Women:	What about the men? They are our strength and pride!
Sergeant:	No, they are pretenders. They pretend to love you; they pretend to care for you, they pretend to fight for you; they pretend to live for you; they even pretend to die for you; they pretend and pretend! So, now, this is your own time. You must pretend they don't exist. The king and the palace are yours.
Ebili:	Umudimkpa, offspring of warriors. Yes?
People *[chorus]*:	Ye-e-e-es!
Ebili:	When a sudden friendship invites a sudden plunge, wary toes must test the depth of the village stream. The defeat of a kingdom is not its smoking ruins; it is when wives forsake

husbands and jostle with daughters to run off with invaders.

[Lance Corporal bursts in breathlessly, thick rope in hand]

Lance Corporal: Shon sir! I have orders to arrest this man! He is wanted back in the palace!

Ebili *[To Sergeant]*: Promotion at last! The palace knows who deserves the palace! Here! *[Holds out his wrists readily to Lance Corporal]*

Lance Corporal: We captured all your chiefs! How far were you going to run?

Ebili: Umudimkpa has seen it full in the eye! Our chiefs are being shamed like captive dogs, our women carried away before our very eyes! Tie me very well, stranger! Tie me very well indeed!

[Blackout]

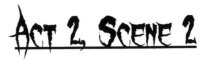

Act 2, Scene 2

Throne room at Umudimkpa palace. Lance Corporal enters, mounts sentry at the door. He is looking stressed and fretful and keeps shifting about, muttering.

Lance Corporal *[aside]*: You hear, you talk, trouble; you hear, no talk, battle. You talk, they ask who tell you. Are names to shout from rooftops? Bad stories tell themselves. They fly without name.

> *[Enter Sergeant. Lance Corporal gesticulates for lowered tones and a safer distance from the king's bedchamber. They step to a corner]*

Sergeant: Ahaa! I hear you were looking everywhere for me?

Lance Corporal: Oga Sergeant, bad word entered my ear . . . . That fine girl of yesterday . . . . Oga Sergeant, bad witch! The king is in danger.

Sergeant *[sternly]*: Who told you that one?

Lance Corporal: Oga Sergeant, they say she is 'man do, man die'.

Sergeant: But the king is up this morning. Didn't they spend the night together?

Lance Corporal: That means another trouble. Unless they were not naked together . . . .

Sergeant: Don't be foolish in your head. Who allows clothes to spoil fun in the dark?

Lance Corporal:	Oga Sergeant, that girl is not fun; she is trouble. They say her future husband put the wicked juju on her body. Naked see her body, man turns into woman.
Sergeant:	What kind of nonsense talk is that?
Lance Corporal:	The king is in danger, Oga Sergeant.
Sergeant:	But Corp'l, what kind of trouble you carried to jam my own head? That girl was your idea!
Lance Corporal:	Ah, Oga Sergeant . . . at all, at all. Only the arrest was my own; not my hand to range her for king!
Sergeant:	Shut up, Lance Corp'l!
Lance Corporal:	Shon sir! I'm still loyal, sir!
Sergeant *[pensive awhile]*:	The trouble is who can trust that Ojongo man . . . I know his type. Big fortune is when a man is sick; they name every small disease by a big sound like the end of this world! Sad but King will not allow a better medicine man . . .

[Enter Abednego]

Abednego:	Come, Sergeant! Where did you pick that girl?
Sergeant:	From her father's house . . . . Shon sir! Good morning, king sir!

[Both men salute Abednego. Sergeant waves Lance Corporal off hastily. Exit Lance Corporal]

Sergeant *[skipping about nervously]*:	Anything wrong, Highness?
Abednego:	The worst night of my life and you pretend to be innocent! But I am the one laughing aloud because you have fallen into my trap, you and that witch. What is what, I have put her in an iron cage. When I finish with both of you, someone will tell me who put it in your head to bring me a witch! Obiora, I'm sure!

[Abednego storms out, leaving Sergeant mystified. Re-enter Lance Corporal, a quizzical look in his anxious eyes]

Lance Corporal: Sarge, the talk is everywhere now . . . . They say the juju on that girl is fire, fire. They say the king cannot be man again! *[whispers]* His man-power can never stand again!

Sergeant: Shut up Corp'l! This man will kill me and you. Think in the head and think fast because me, I will kill you first!

Lance Corporal: Oga Sergeant, plenty women came from Big City. Give permit, they enter today, today . . . . Fine, fine girls to change everything!

Sergeant: Are you thinking at all? More girls, more nothing for king! More trouble for you and me!

Lance Corporal: Oga Sergeant, city girls are city girls. Not like native women who only know to get pregnant. Fine girls from Big City! They move sharp.

Sergeant: Bring a sample, Corp'l. Quick, three or four . . . and various sizes!

[Exeunt both in different directions. A flute is heard in a deeply stirring rendition]

Flute: Akweke olima, Akw'eke olima
   (O purest gem, O rarest gem)
Dooh olimaima, dooh olima
   (A lament for my precious gem)
Akweke olima, Akw'eke olima
   (O purest gem, O rarest gem)
Dooh olimaima, dooh olima
   (A lament for my precious gem)
Akw'eke m'debelu n'onwo n'ozurozi
   (Precious gem that I'd so carefully stowed away is all but gone)
Dooh olimaima dooh olima
   (A lament for my precious gem)

[Enter Abednego shaking with rage, shouting]

Abednego *[to nobody]*: Who allowed that flute? Who is blowing it? Stop that idiot immediately! Guards! Guards!

[Constables 2 and 3 enter and freeze in attention]

Abednego: That tune is banned with immediate effect! I forbid the sound of it and the name in it in this palace, until further notice!

[Abednego turns sharply to go but stops abruptly]

Constable 2: Shon, sir! We shall enforce straightaway.

Abednego: Wait! Not so fast! I suspect you. Where were you last night? You were peeping! That's it! You were peeping!

Constable 2: Peeping?

Constable 3: King, we are trained policemen; we never peep unless there is a threat to security! Love is no threat to security though love stories fly like sparrows and everyone talks like he witnessed everything.

Constable 2: And the fastest story is when royalty meets romance . . . .

Abednego: Romance! Who permitted you to put your eyes in my affairs? Security, security, but what about my privacy?

Constable 3: King, sir, you gave orders that the king's security is first always.

Abednego: So, that's your excuse to do bad things—what we did as little children—stand by the door and peep through the door hole!

Constables 3: I swear that nobody peeped, Your Highness. Nobody peeped!

Abednego:	I know you peeped! What annoys me is what were you looking for? What did you want to see? Whether your king is a man or what?
Constable 3:	Your Highness, this is a strange accusation . . . .
Abednego:	Accusation, he says! Go and ask of me at Ubulu and other places, who I am, how many women! Find out in the open, you stupid nosy creeps! Why door holes?
Constable 3:	Not door holes, Your Highness. We can kill any gossip for you.
Abednego:	What do you know about killing gossip? By your own admission everybody already knows? What does that tell you?
Constable 1:	King, sir . . . .
Abednego:	What that tells me is that people have to die . . . . or the paramount ruler becomes a paramount joke. Go and think in the head. When you come back, tell me why people should not be killed. Starting with both of you!

[Exeunt Constables 2 and 3 in mad haste]

Abednego *[shouting at their backs]*:	And stop that flute! Somebody, stop that madness on a flute, now!

[Enter Akweke, smiling and gyrating]

Akweke *[hissing]*:	See who thinks he can stop my song!
Abednego:	You again? How did you manage to come out again?
Akweke:	I warned you I'm a witch. When I strip, nothing stands!
	[She takes a tentative step, arms outstretched towards Abednego but he backs off with evident apprehension]
Akweke:	Shall I strip again?

Abednego: Keep away from me!

                     [Akweke performs a weird gyration. Lights dim]

Akweke: Sing my song for me . . . Sing . . . like last night . . . Did you not want something? Why are you running from it? This is me, Akweke . . . precious Egg of the sacred python, the silent one of the Agbala shrine . . . Come and take what you wanted . . . . Come . . . .

Abednego *[backing further away, grabs a big stick]*:   Keep away from me! Keep away or I will break your head!

Akweke: Agbala will ask questions . . . . Come, this is my human head . . . the human head of a sacred python. Break it! Break the head of the daughter of a spirit that touched nothing of yours.

Abednego *[badly shaken]*: Guards! Guards!

Akweke: Why are you calling for help? I am only an egg! Can't you see? Only an egg . . . Akweke . . . .

Abednego: Gua-a-a-ards!

                     [Constables 2 and 3 rush in; Akweke squats, sings]

Akweke: Akweke olima, Akw'eke olima
                     Dooh olimaima, dooh olima
                     Akweke olima, Akw'eke olima
                     Dooh olimaima, dooh olima

                     [Constables stand confused, staring]

Abednego *[screaming nervously]*: Take away this evil! She's a witch!

Akweke *[rising]*:   You goats of the wilderness! Let one of you dare touch me! I will strip for your mothers to cry!

Constable 2 *[recoiling]*: Ah! A witch?

Akweke *[singing]*: Akweke olima, Akw'eke olima
                     Dooh olimaima, dooh olima

Akweke olima, Akw'eke olima
Dooh olimaima, dooh olima

[Enter Ebili, promptly plays on his flute. Akweke dances untidily, everyone stepping back from her]

Constable 3: A witch!

Abednego: Fetch Ojongo from my bedchamber. Tell him to come quickly!

[The constables dash in and out of the bedchamber]

Constable 2: He is not there.

Abednego *[resignedly]*: That's how they are and who they are . . . Never there when you need them most! *[Furiously]* Ojongo! Ojongo!

Akweke: Akweke olima, Akw'eke olima
(O purest gem, O rarest gem)
Dooh olimaima, dooh olima
(A lament for my precious gem)

Abednego: Ojongo!

[Akweke glides to a halt and stoops before the throne]

Akweke: Umudimkpa salutes the repeat talk of mother hen
The daily feast of clicks and clucks that grows the brood
Not everything that crows like cock is mate or male
Nor is every shiny grain a meal for he-lizard
The fly that follows fancies may end up in a flame.
A river cannot hide because moon face is blood
It is a mild race if a woman minds her breasts;
In a race for dear life, the flappers fly unchecked.

Abednego *[in rage]*: Why are you dumb like donkeys? Grab this witch and throw her back in the cell!

[Enter Ojongo, twisting, shaking and grunting]

Ojongo: Touch her not! She will go on her own.

- 86 -

Abednego [*furiously*]:   Ojongo, where did you go? Where were you?

Ojongo: The spirits so quick to summon me to their cave in the hills much quicker returned me here in time. Let every goat be warned that not every grass is common crop. [*Shakes much more*] That girl is no grazing field. Great One, let her go!

Abednego: I am the one who gives orders here and she has a lot to answer to. Spirit or human, she stays detained and that is final.

    [*A general stir and nervous shifting, everyone stepping back as Akweke dances some provocative 'mpete' steps. Ebili shadows her with a spritely serenade on his flute*]

Ojongo: Ojongo may not ask the cause of a fight or the purpose of a feast. But when a bitter tale is filling my mouth, the prudent ear must hear. The fire that will burn down a house seldom gives a sign. I see warrior masks before me dancing dangerous steps. Not every cub on four legs is a playmate for baby dog.

Abednego: If it is about this odious witch, forget your fancy talk. She must be tied with the father of ropes and sent back to her cell. And I am putting that cell under my personal watch!

Ojongo: Great One . . . . the strength of a basket is not in catching smoke!

Abednego: You are letting a common frog defy my powers. She jumps about in my face but all you do is fill my royal ears with noises and silly threats! And where are my guards? I have no real guards, only expensive idiots who cannot be trusted to mind their own skulls! But all of you, wait for my hand and see!

Ojongo: Leave us alone, everybody, leave me and Great One . . . . For whoever tarries, the eye that lingers shall sorrow in blindness.

Abednego *[to the constables]*:   Tie up that witch and put her right back in her cell. And be sure to use the monster locks, or both of you are the next fools to die by my hands!

> *[Exeunt Akweke and Ebili, the constables following]*

Ojongo: Great One . . . .

Abednego: Don't make me regret you, Ojongo. I will not fear a baby girl of yesterday because of some juju powder that she sprinkled on herself. Why do I have you as a medicine man?

> *[Abednego storms back into his bedchamber. Ojongo stands mulling the situation. Enter Oyidi'a, an earthen bowl in hand]*

Ojongo *[flustered, warms up]*:   Mother of all . . . . *[laughs to please]* Mother of all!

> *[Oyidi'a thoroughly ignores him and inches on with the pained slight stoop of an octogenarian]*

Ojongo: Mother of all . . . *[ingratiating]* it is Ojongo . . . . I offer greetings.

Oyidi'a *[vehemently]*:   Tufiaa! *[A pause and then more vehemently, eyes closed]* Again, I say 'Tufia!' *[With much more vehemence]* The only salute to abomination is 'Tufiaa!'

> *[Ojongo slinks away and exits. Oyidi'a slowly hobbles towards the throne. Enter Lance Corporal]*

Lance Corporal *[rushing to stop Oyidi'a]*: You again, old woman! I told you where to wait; you must stay there with the others. *[Oyidi'a ignores him and carries on.]* You cannot enter without permit! King is not seeing people. Didn't I tell you? I told you!

[Oyidi'a finds a way around him. Enter Sergeant]

Lance Corporal: Shon sir! I told this one! I told her king is not seeing anybody.

[Oyidi'a stands silent before the throne and slowly flings pinches of chalk powder at it.]

Sergeant: Old woman, old woman! Do you have paper for that your work? Show me your gorment permit or no work!

Lance Corporal: Oga, this is my trouble with old people! They never hear when they don't want to hear! Beat them a little, everybody will begin to shout and say "have you no father, no mother?" I told her "wait for clearance!" Simple word!

[Echezo appears in the doorway]

Echezo: The queen and mother of the whole kingdom will never need anybody's clearance to stand before the throne of her own husband.

Sergeant: And who are you, yourself? Who allowed you here?

Echezo: I am Echezo, headman of the palace attendants. If I wasn't dragged away from duty post to prison last night, I should be the one asking the questions . . .

Sergeant: Get lost before I open my eyes. If I count three and still find you here, you will be arrested as a spy!

Echezo: Do away with anyone you call spy; but don't ever hinder this woman from her duty to the gods.

Sergeant: What duty? What nonsense duty?

Echezo: The duty she has performed every single day for the past seventy years . . . and it is no nonsense!

[Oyidi'a rounds up her silent ministrations, paying no heed to anyone; she slowly heads for the exit]

Lance Corporal *[whistles sharply and exclaims in a hushed tone]*:

Seventy years! The mother of my own mother was yet unborn!

Echezo: That's how long that amazing lady has done what you've just witnessed. She is the first and only surviving wife of Igwe, the great Sky-king of Umudimkpa who is our reigning monarch. This palace is her own home. Please show her some respect.

Sergeant: Someone, help my curiosity—I'm a stranger in these parts. If what we hear is true, that woman gave your king no son to sit on the empty throne. That is the root of all your trouble. Why does the whole kingdom worship her like a goddess?

Echezo: Because that is what she is, a living goddess . . . . a woman without blemish. Nobody remembers the reproach of her womb because she is a mother to every son and daughter of Umudimkpa. She bears our hope, the hope of the whole nation that a true-born of the Sky-king is coming to sit on this throne someday.

Sergeant: That is one pipe dream that the hand of your own gods has put out like smoke. A real person has entered this palace, not a dream but a true son of the soil. He has taken the throne and your people should be dancing in the square if they know what is good for them! You have a living king, not a dead dream!

Lance Corporal: Even the gods are ready; they will dance at his coronation.

Echezo:	Careless talk is cheap in a stranger's mouth but fatal to a native ear.
Sergeant:	What was that you just said?
Echezo:	Just a prayer to the gods for punishment of folly to spare me and you if some intended fun has sounded like foolishness!

[Exit Echezo]

Sergeant:	Follow that man and throw him out of the premises. When are those girls coming?
Lance Corporal:	Shon sir! The palace will be full now, now. Trust me, sir!

[Exeunt Lance Corporal and Sergeant in opposite directions . . . . . . Fade]

ACT 2, SCENE 3

Throne Room at the palace of Umudimkpa. Abednego, irritable and listless, comes in from his bedchamber, followed by a solicitous Ojongo.

Ojongo:	We have to talk, Great One.
Abednego:	The talk is enough. Do something, Ojongo! I am supposed to be king and I have you; yet nothing is standing or working!
Ojongo:	Isn't that why we must talk? Delay is unkind to the grand outing of the awaited masquerade. It is time to face Akaeze.
Abednego:	I am not ready for that irritant yet.
Ojongo:	I have something to make you ready. When you hold it in your hand, no power in this world can look you in the eye.
Abednego:	Bring what you have and let me see.
	[Exit Ojongo. Enter three brightly costumed belles who begin to dance seductively around Abednego]
Abednego:	Sweethearts, sweethearts, you must wait . . . . a little longer!
Belles:	For how long? You've kept us waiting for ever. It's unfair.
Abednego:	See, I've been too busy.
Belles:	Busy is the excuse of eunuchs and failing husbands. But you are different. We know you are different.

Abedznego: Sweethearts, it is not easy to be king. Too many important things to do and too many useless people to see . . . . Even the high chiefs have been waiting for days . . . . no time to see them.

Belles: High chiefs or low chiefs, they can wait. We can't.

[Wriggling to the melody of a love song, they begin to slowly strip and tease, pulling Abednego to a corner. Re-enter Ojongo]

Ojongo: And whose daughters are these ones?

Abednego: City women, Ojongo . . . . And, take it as you see it, daughters of men do not suffer the names of their fathers in the cities.

Ojongo: They clearly don't endure the dresses of their mothers either!

Abednego: Ojongo, watch your eyes for stolen pleasures. Overlook charms which are not in your own line of trade.

Ojongo: Not my business but spirit or human, everything has a name.

[The half nudes waltz, pirouette and cavort about]

First belle: Just call me Kiki . . . . Just Kiki!

Second belle: Me, I'm Zizi . . . . Zizi!.

Third belle: And me, I'm Pimpim!

Ojongo *[aside]*: Envy of dogs is what it sounds like in my ears! But everything they call fashion these days is straight from dogs!

Abednego *[watching the girls hum and sway before him]*: Ojongo, these are modern times, and modern things are what you see happening here . . . Umudimkpa under me will open up like the big cities, women never in short supply. They will come in thousands when they hear I am king. These ones are just the early birds . . . .

Belles *[giggling]*: We want to be first lady like every woman. First lady!

Abednego: Sweethearts, the king and the kingdom are safe in your hands!

[The tune changes to Afro beat; the girls dance in turns]

Zizi: So, come and dance with us the dance of safest hands.

Pimpim: A dance of hills and valleys and the swirling ponds.

Kiki: A dance of pumpkin leaves . . .

Pimipim: Of tendrils fresh, of bold creepers and their bulging gourds . . . .

Zizi: Come dance with us, dance . . . . dance . . . .
[Drags Abednego into a dance. He sways awhile but stiffens abruptly. The music stops too, the lights dimming; a melancholic tune plays]

Abednego: My moment shall arise; it's then I'll go with you
To the distance of rainbows and the dimpled riverbed
And thickly woods, split open to a shaft of lightning,
Will trap laughter of thunder in the womb of sunrise . . . .

Pimpim: Empty words yet again! It's so unlike you!

Zizi: What is a rush of words when a woman just needs her man?

Kiki: Like the drumbeat is again for nothing. Like you are avoiding us

Zizi: Are we not pleasing anymore to our king?

Abednego *[much depressed]*:   Just go, for now, girls; go, for now . . . . please go.

Zizi: That word is strange in your mouth. I never heard you say please before.

Abednego *[wearily]*:   You must leave . . . . I have many things troubling my mind. You have no idea. I need some time . . . But I will see you . . . . later . . .

Pimpim: This is serious . . . . What can we say? We shall keep waiting.

Kiki: Do we have a choice?

Pimpim: Girls, it's a long and gloomy night, hope of dawn our only light.

[The girls pick up their dress items sullenly. Exeunt]

Ojongo *[holds out a short carved stick]*:   This is power to face down giants and make mountains to tremble before you.

Abednego: What I need is different! And you ought to know that! If you can't make it happen, count your days as few!

[He storms out, leaving Ojongo bewildered . . . . Fade]

Act 2, Scene 4

Throne Room at Umudimkpa palace. The throne is covered with a heavy black cloth firmly tied to it with a rough cord; all stools have been removed, including the queen's. An antiquated hard-backed chair on the fore part of the dais faces a stretch of low wooden benches ranging end-to-end across the floor and against the two side walls. Lance Corporal is standing dejectedly in the corner, both arms folded like a heavy burden atop his head as Ojongo and Sergeant deliberate with an awe-stricken Abednego on the other side of the room. A flute resounds somewhere on the palace grounds.

Flute/voice-over: If spittle is sport, the joke is not on serpent
Surprise, surprise! Sizzle, frizzle! Twitch!

Sergeant *[indicating Lance Corporal]:* He was the one on duty!

Ojongo *[dirty chuckle]:* Duty! What is called duty?

Abednego: Ojongo . . . .

Ojongo *[quickly covers Abednego's mouth with his hand]:* Not a word, Great One, not a word! This is an evil trap, the hand of your enemies! But Ojongo is here for you!

Sergeant: King sir, this thing must be properly investigated!

Ojongo *[sneering]:* Investigated! What is called investigated?

Sergeant: King, this juju cloth did not fall from the sky. Somebody's hand put it there and removed the chairs of the chiefs. I must investigate. Everybody is a suspect! Everybody!

Abednego *[puzzled]:* Ojongo . . . . .

Ojongo [shuts Abednego's mouth again with a quick hand]: No word, Great
One. I must put thunder in your mouth before
you speak again. Your enemies have gone so far
they must now be taught a serious lesson! Let
this one stand there and be talking investigated!
[Mimics Sergeant in his face] Everybody is a
suspect!

[Ojongo steers Abednego off the stage into the
bedroom, Sergeant following uncertainly]

Lance Corporal [aside, morosely]: I am undone! They have finished
me!

[Enter Constable 3]

Constable 3: But Corp'l, you were on duty. It's strange for
all this to happen, yet you saw nobody and you
heard nothing!

Lance Corporal [flaring up]: Anybody can come and blame me
because blame is cheap. But hear the owners of
the land! They say area spirits do things like this
and nobody can see them!

Constable 3: The big trouble this time is that king is too
angry. That black cloth is like death is the owner
of the throne.

Lance Corporal: Somebody is my enemy here! They just want to
finish me off!

Constable 3 [shrugs indifferently]: Big trouble!

[Exit Lance Corporal. The flute resonates. Enter
Akaeze and Oyidia led by Constables 1 and 2.
They settle dispiritedly on a bench against the
side wall]

Flute/voice-over: If palm nuts are ripening at the tip of fronds
If roasted yam has sprouted fresh tendrils
If roosters become layers of chicken eggs
Whose tested tongue can tell the tufted tale?
Surprise, surprise, sizzle, frizzle! Twitch!

[*Akaeze and Oyidi'a remain deep in silence, heads bowed. The three constables just out of earshot, converse in low whispers, stroking their batons*]

Constable 1:   Mates, we have to be careful with these ones . . .

Constable 3:   When old people are refusing to die, every moment in their presence is like graveside. It makes you feel like an undertaker!

Constable 2:   These ones have the deepest respect of their people. The man is their Prime Minister; the lady is Queen. Let's be careful.

Constable 1:   I don't even know which one is worse, their silence of stone or the eloquence of pain in their weary eyes.

Constable 3:   Orders are orders, mates. Are we going to fall for the tricks of old age and fail the king? Let's do something quick!

Constable 2:   Like what?

Constable 3:   Like beat them on their bare backsides! They must talk!

Constable 1:   Ah! Another egg could break in our hands. That is the life of aged folks; it is like temptation, fragile and thin. Death is always a hair's breadth away.

Constable 2:   We already have the problem of that ageless one, Ochilize who collapsed in detention. He went on to die; did you not hear?

Constable 1:   I heard. Who hasn't heard? Correct name is Oche-ilo-eze. I fear more reprisal attacks.

Constable 3:   They do their reprisal, we do our own. Who *born* dog?

Constable 2:   We cannot afford this bloodbath to go on. It is plain madness and must stop.

Constable 3:	How can it stop? These natives are impossible! See their ancients like dumb statues, refusing to talk peace!
Constable 1:	Is it their fault that we bring them here every day but King is playing a strange game? Old people can be stubborn too.
Constable 2:	So, who carried away the chairs? And who put black cloth on the king's throne?
Constable 1:	Leave that matter because it is a spirit matter for king and his own people. Corp'l is the one I pity; it happened in his watch.
Constable 3:	Somebody answer me. Are we beating these old ones or not?
Constable 2:	King said we must make them talk today.
Constable 3:	Enough of talk-talk. They refuse to talk. What do we do?

[The flute renders a short, sharp threnody]

Constable 1:	Our friend never tires on his flute. Can he be the native cricket who becomes lead singer when cockerels fall asleep?

[They cock their ears to the sad lament of the flute]

Constable 2:	I think we should bring him here to sit with these ones.
Constable 3:	He can join them and when they talk, we open our ears.

[Exeunt the constables, the flute reeling crisp notes]

Flute/voice-over:	Surprise, surprise! Sizzle, frizzle! Twitch! If farmhouse hen has grown sharp biting teeth Surprise, surprise! Sizzle, frizzle! Twitch! If he-goat returns pregnant, full with child Surprise, surprise! Sizzle, frizzle! Twitch!

If a new-born child stands up and walks a
mile . . .
Surprise, surprise! Sizzle, frizzle! Twitch!
What shocking scene can make an eye to bleed?
Surprise, surprise! Sizzle, frizzle! Twitch!
The heavy rain that beats a log is just another
bath!

[Enter Sergeant, looking very agitated]

Sergeant: Corp'l, where are you? Corp'l!

[Re-enter Lance Corporal]

Lance Corporal: Shon sir!

Sergeant *[brusquely]:*   Clear this room quickly. We must talk.

*[He paces as Lance Corporal frets with Akaeze
& Oyidi'a who finally rise and leave impassively,
Lance Corporal seeing them out and hurrying
back]*

Lance Corporal: Shon sir!

Sergeant: King is very angry. Either I kick you out or he
will kick me out!

Lance Corporal *[kneeling instantly]:*   Oga Sergeant, why this thing
happened, I swear. It was sake of my up and
down for king and the girls! One minute is come
here, next minute go there.

Sergeant: There is no time for baby talk, Corp'l. Get up.
King will soon come out and he will ask you one
last time. Talk like a man.

Lance Corporal *[rising to his feet, resignedly]:*   Ah, my enemies have
used a wicked hand to knock my head! What
can I say to king?

Sergeant: Think in the head; talk like a man. Who are
your own suspects?

Lance Corporal:	My mind is confused . . . but what I suspect is that medicine man.
Sergeant:	Who? Ojongo? Why?
Lance Corporal:	Because juju men will first make you fear, and then they make charms for the fear you fear . . . and you must pay every time.
Sergeant:	Corp'l, would you be as stupid as you look in the face? King will never listen to this kind of story! You must tell him what he can believe . . . I have a good lie, but it will cost you a big amount.
Lance Corporal:	If it is money, I will pay at month end, Oga Sergeant. I will pay.
Sergeant:	Your wages for this month . . . . . or you alone, carry your trouble.
Lance Corporal:	Please, Oga! *[Resignedly]* Take all the money but help me . . . . *[He follows Sergeant as he drifts slightly away]*
Sergeant *[furtively]*:	Fine! I will help you as you are loyal. Go and tell Ojongo that both of us actually saw the person who did this thing.
Lance Corporal:	We saw who, sir?
Sergeant:	Is it not that old chief, the one they call Akaeze?
Lance Corporal:	Ah! Sergeant . . . . Who will believe us?
Sergeant:	People believe lies and only argue with truth. Tell Ojongo that we saw the old chief with our own eyes. He brought some very old women all dressed in white and they blew the stools away like this . . . . *[makes a crude chewing noise and blows out]*

Lance Corporal *[rehearses the chewing and blowing]:*   But . . . Sergeant, Ojongo will run to king; and king would ask why we did not shout!

Sergeant:	Think in the head, Corp'l. Those women came stark naked with charms that roared like lions. Everywhere was covered with thick smoke . . . and *fiam!* It was over in a twinkling of an eye. Am I wrong, Corp'l?
Lance Corporal:	No, Oga Sergeant. That is how it happened but I forgot in my head. Thank you for remembering for me, sir. Shon sir!
Sergeant:	Now, Corp'l, get your girls! They should start misbehaving well around here. Let's see their magic the way you boasted.
Lance Corporal:	Oga Sergeant, you will see correct show now, now, now.

[Enter Constable 1, waits till Lance Corporal exits]

Constable 1 *[earnestly]*:	Shon, sir! Sergeant, I feel I should talk to you in private. It is urgent! *[Lowers his voice]* A very bad story is spreading everywhere about king and the witch girl. It is very damaging . . . .

[Abednego's voice is heard coming from his chamber. They both stiffen, then hide in the corner. Enter Abednego and Ojongo]

Abednego:	I paid you a fortune and it is for performance, not promises. All I need from you and the spirits is power to sit on the throne of our fathers and be a man in every respect!
Ojongo:	Nobody can do what Ojongo has already done for you!
Abednego:	What have you done that I cannot feel in my body? I need to be a man, a strong man!
Ojongo:	I warned you that your enemies are not resting! This job is not for the loose waist strings you call policemen. This is war!

Abednego:	Just face your own side! Stop quarrelling with my guards!
Ojongo:	You are putting your life in the hands of jokers who cannot protect even their own noses from the birds of night! Which one of them can tell us who carried the chiefs' stools from this palace or who put a black cloth on the throne? This is a war that only Ojongo knows how to fight!
Abednego:	That is why I hired you! I must win or I wipe out this kingdom!
Ojongo:	Ojongo knows what to do. *[He spreads his mat on the floor. Lights go dimmer as he sits.]* In a short while, my herbs will sigh in the log fire; then, smoke in your nostrils shall be freedom, the hunter to follow the sharp point of his spear.
	[He rummages through his goatskin bag and lays various effigies and objects before him on the mat. Abednego, looking nervous, hurries over to squat opposite him on the same mat]
Abednego:	Ojongo, I have no more interest in bland proverbs . . . . everything is down, refusing to stand up. Nothing is working . . . . it is very embarrassing! What is a leopard without his vitality?
Ojongo:	Ojongo is here before you. Make yourself clear. What is the problem?
Abednego:	You are the one that should tell me the problem. This is a nightmare. Everything just went down. It doesn't make sense to me. I can't even say it in words.
Ojongo:	But you must talk. If you don't talk, the spirits would suppose I am only meddling. Why should I disturb the peace of the gods with a complaint from nobody?

Abednego:	Ojongo, this matter is very embarrassing to me. How am I to say what you will understand in exactly how I feel? See, don't you know the strength of battle in a battle spear?
Ojongo *[reflects and nods uncertainly]*:	In a battle spear . . . .
Abednego:	Full of strength! That's it, Ojongo! Or kingdom means nothing!
Ojongo:	Strength is strength, surely.
Abednego:	That's my point, see? So, why is everything suddenly down like that?
Ojongo:	Down like how?
Abednego:	Like I'm telling you! What kind of nonsense is that? I want you to put everything straight and strong without delay!
Ojongo:	Ojongo is seated. Darkness is never afraid of shadows. The hunter should be the happiest guest at a feast of antelopes.
Abednego:	Where is my joy, Ojongo? I doubt you even understand what I am trying to tell you. See, have you ever climbed a tree, the fruits ripe and ready, but your hand is not reaching out to pluck any? You are hungry and staring at a meal but you cannot get yourself up to eat it?
Ojongo:	It is this battle against your coronation! The wicked hand of your enemies is everywhere.
Abednego:	Why am I hearing this same talk every time?
Ojongo:	Your enemies are not ordinary mortals. They have deployed extremely powerful forces to hit you front and back. What they've sent this time, it is an evil fog . . . They want to confuse and torment not only you but everyone around you . . . but they forgot something! Ojongo, the terrible hawk is sitting here now and watching everyone that is watching you!

Abednego:	I paid you all you demanded in money, livestock, everything . . . . Things must move . . . . and whatever should stand up must stand up quick. I must be strong; I need to break every protocol that constrains my freedom. I am a man, and king I am!
Ojongo:	Ojongo asks you to name your wish. Say it in direct words.
Abednego *[puffs his cheeks, exasperated]*:	I will say no more than I have already said. But I must see an immediate change. In fact, I think the answer is to begin to sit on that throne. Yes, the throne! *[He rises abruptly and moves toward the throne]*
Ojongo *[springing to his feet, shaking]*:	Hmmm! Let all earth be witness that I warned you against that throne.
Abednego:	I refuse to buy cheap warnings. The king's throne is good for my confidence . . . and my power . . . . and my strength as a man!
Ojongo:	Hear me, Great One; ancient caps have their headaches and ancient stools their pricks and pains. Why must you sit where enemies are waiting for you to sit? Do you think it is wisdom?
Abednego:	I hired you to make my rear parts strong. I must be able to sit anywhere I want.
Ojongo:	Would you sit on egg because you can? Or on another man's shit because your buttocks are bigger?
Abednego:	A king sits on the throne. I will not be king and fear the king's throne!
Ojongo:	If you would get down with me on the mat, we shall hear from the oracles . . . . *[returns to his mat, shuffles his divining pebbles, peers at them. Abednego resumes squatting]* The spirits ask which one makes the other, the king or the throne.

	Won't a common stool become a throne when a king is seated on it?
Abednego:	Tell the spirits that where there is a throne of countless ages, a king is foolish to sit on something else. Every king before me sat on that special throne. It gave them strength as men of power. Why should my case be different?
Ojongo:	Every king before you was the offspring of the man who sat there before him. Only the gods know why nobody has sat there for these twenty years. Make your own throne where you can sit without pain.
Abednego:	Umudimkpa would mock. If I build myself a different throne, they would say 'Aha! He is afraid.'
Ojongo:	Afraid of whom? The whole world knows that Ojongo is behind you; and Ojongo never drums for a weak-minded masquerade. Who would mock you for sitting on a new throne so beautiful it says 'shut up' to this old one?
Abednego:	Ojongo, I paid you a fortune to give me results, not arguments. That throne is a symbol and there is a power in it that I desire for myself. I need it as a man! Give it to me without excuses!

[Ojongo shuffles and examines his divining cowries]

Ojongo:	Hmmm! Your imminent coronation is a war that has raised all the deities from their sleep. Can you see what I see? There will be spirit mines and missiles on a scale never witnessed in these parts. But Ojongo is ready to parboil you against mishap.
Abednego:	That is what I paid you for. I want to face and conquer, not shrink and avoid. A scorpion cannot fear the buzz of a cockroach or the many

	feet of a millipede. So, stop your mind games and name your price! I am ready to pay anything for what I want—and I mean, any price!
Ojongo:	Does that include your own life?
Abednego:	You and I know the rule is substitution. How many heads for mine?

[Ojongo cackles, goes pensive, examines various objects]

Ojongo:	Choi! Choi!! Seasons and arrivals! Choi! I hear the noises; the wind is full of threats and warnings. Choi! There is no sound of laughter in the coming rain. Choi! Choi! It is only in the land of do-nothing men that rumours are louder than the battle itself. Choi!! Tell the wise, he will hear; tell the wayward, he goes shaking his head till he shakes it off in the bush! The fluttering thing that mocks a sitting toad at lunch-time must not land as a winged insect. Hmmm! Ah! Strong Head that asked Ojongo to do something, are you prepared to hear this one?
Abednego:	My heart is strong. I will pay any price, even human heads!
Ojongo:	The spirits are not talking of human heads.
Abednego:	What do they want?
Ojongo:	They are talking . . . . of something else and someone important . . . . Someone very, very important in this land . . . But the gods cannot be denied . . . You will never deny the gods!
Abednego:	What do they want?
Ojongo:	Hmmm! The name is loud in my ear . . . . .
Abednego:	Speak it in mine.
Ojongo:	It is Oyidi'a, Mother of all.

[*In their hiding place, the two policemen are horrified*]

Abednego: Ah, High Mother . . . That's some pity! But, she has lived long enough, even over-lived! If the spirits want her head, well!

Ojongo: It is not her head they want! Their talk is of something else.

Abednego: What?

Ojongo: They say she must give her full consent.

Abednego: How? She is even more hostile now than Akaeze and their fine boy, Obiora!

Ojongo: Hostile?

Abednego: Very hostile! Since I brought them out of detention, she has turned herself into a cold stone, refusing to talk to me or even look my way. What can I say to ever please her?

Ojongo: Not words, Great One. You cannot sit on that throne unless . . .

Abednego: Unless what?

Ojongo: Unless you lie with her as man with a woman.

Abednego [*on his feet in shock and disgust*]: The gods should be ashamed of themselves!

Ojongo: Watch your tongue!

Abednego: You too watch it! Are you insane? That woman is . . . is . . . Older than my late grandmother.

Ojongo: That throne is much older than her.

Abednego: There must be another way. There has to be another way!

Ojongo: The gods forbid argument. You are the one who wants results.

Abednego:	But . . . She won't even let me come near her . . . and I really can't touch . . . . her . . . . Not at her age! Not in that way!
Ojongo:	Ojongo knows what to do if he is asked to do something.
Abednego:	Come, come, this is not something another ear should hear. Let's talk in the sure privacy of my bedchamber.

[Exit Abednego. Ojongo, humming a tune, gathers his stuff into his goatskin bag, rolls up his mat]

Ojongo *[aside]:*	Let me hear more '*Tufiaa*' from up sky!

[Exit Ojongo. In the dim light, Sergeant and Constable 1 emerge from their hiding place, shocked beyond words]

Constable 1:	Oga Sergeant, I can't believe my ears!
Sergeant *[holding a silencing finger to his lips]:*	Best to play dumb. Best a dumb mute always, to hear the deeps!
Constable 1:	Men can do anything to be king in this world! My father used to say it, that power is like moonshine. The madness in every dog comes awake at full moon!
Sergeant:	Leave dogs alone, my good friend. Madness at moonshine is worse in men.
Constable 1:	The heavens have saved the land from shame as one rod of madness that knows no control has been put down. May it never rise again!
Sergeant:	Careful with your tongue. The walls have ears.

[Exit Sergeant on tip-toes; Constable 1 dithers, then follows]

[Fade]

Act 3, Scene 1

Throne room at Umudimkpa Palace, the throne still hooded in black and all the high stools gone. Three belles, clutching knee-length loosened wrappers over their bare chests, stand whispering and giggling.

Kiki: What I can see is—his people are very jealous of him. They don't like him at all; that's why they were lying to us that his own is finished! Lies upon lies! The man is thunder!

Zizi: But he too was behaving funny even up to yesterday, like it was true.

Pimpim: What I hear is, there was a true leg in the story. They say everything changed later because of that *baba*.

Kiki: Same I heard. They said the *baba* came and did something.

Zizi: The something is too much. No stop, no wait! The man will kill somebody!

             [A fourth belle bursts out of the bedchamber, gasping. The rest begin to mimic her limp but she hurries off as Abednego's trailing voice calls for her return]

Abednego's voice: Hey, pretty one! Come back! Don't disobey your king like that! Come back here or be arrested! It is an order!

             [The others tip-toe to hurry off but Constable 3 enters]

Constable 3 *[blocks their exit]*:   King is calling you! Orders are orders, go back!

Kiki *[conspiratorially]*:   Just advise king to rest a little! Rest is good for kings.

Zizi *[cynically]*:   Let's advise him direct, girls . . . Let's tell him to take a rest. What do you say, girls?

All together: Take a rest, King. Bye! *[The girls run off, giggling]*

Constable 3 *[aside]*:   King, sir, if ever you need a little help, *[pauses dramatically, then shouts, beating his chest]* I'm here, friend!

[Enter Ojongo, bowl in hand]

Ojongo: Which friend is your own?

Constable 3:   Ah, Great Hand of the mighty spirits, greetings! Just a mad joy of the heart saluting a crazy wish of the head, a poor man forgets himself altogether!

Ojongo: You may not be twice lucky. That's how it often starts!

Constable 3:   I was only celebrating what your hand has done. We saw with our own eyes. Mighty One, give me my own share of this stuff that has turned the whole kingdom on its head!

Ojongo: Ojongo knows what to do if your own fist is not clenched.

Constable 3:   I swear to see you at month end. I know what I like.

Ojongo: The rush is not waiting till month end. Sweetmeat is never reserved for latecomers.

Constable 3:   If I miss out, you are the one who made me kill for it.

Ojongo *[chuckles]*:   Same talk from your senior colleagues! Very, very soon, one of you will kill the rest of you! Ha!

[Constable 3 quickly makes way. Exit Ojongo, going past him towards the king's bedchamber]

Ojongo *[a loud knock, shouting within]:* Great One, the last pot is at your doorstep and it brings you my fullest greetings!

Abednego *[shouting within]:* Wait! The king shall put on clothes and emerge.

[Ojongo re-enters, humming a tune. Exit Constable 3.]

Ojongo *[aside]:* It is not a common hawk that lifted his wings and the market fell silent. Sunrise derided the village head as a childless fool; Sunset is begging him to disperse his countless offspring from the thoroughfare! Choi!

[Enter Abednego, gleefully flexing his muscles]

Abednego: O-jongo! This earth can never be carried out of its place! Stampede or tumult, iroko is iroko! Look at me, Ojongo! I am the strength of seven bulls and seven rivers! Mountains are nothing; canyons are a lie! Let tomorrow happen today!

Ojongo: Ojongo knows what every leaf in the forest is saying to the sky.

Abednego: I hear their language of power in my blood. It is the force of running brooks that no power can swim against. I am a new force, Ojongo!

Ojongo: Here is the fifth and final pot. After this doze, every woman is bush meat in your hands and you may range and roam as you please . . . . There is only one condition.

Abednego *[frowns, suspicious]:* What condition?

Ojongo: The boundary no man should cross . . . . Married women.

Abednego *[dismissively]:* I hear that all the time.

Ojongo:	This time, it is different. You cannot touch any woman whose head carries a dowry paid by another man who is still alive.
Abednego *[aside]:*	The sooner the widows!
	[produces a small gourd from his waist cloth, shakes its dark powdery content into the offered bowl]
Ojongo:	Potent spices?
Abednego:	Regard it as salt . . . . for better taste. You drink first!
	[He makes Ojongo gulp a massive test doze, then he sips]
Abednego:	What is your own fever against married women?
Ojongo:	They are forbidden . . . . by reason and religion as by the custom of races and the content of this bowl. When you drink this final potion, you must never touch another man's wife. I never do.
	[Abednego paces a bit uncomfortably, the bowl in hand]
Abednego:	What happens if I do? No, don't bother to remix those tales and threats they poured into my ears from early boyhood. They are nothing to me, just cheap concoctions to scare a strongman from the fullest conquests of his destiny!
Ojongo:	Destiny has its fine song, Great One. But the last ear of stubbornness is usually the first gate of untimely death. And self-destruction is the common lot of the wild he-goat who shows no respect for set boundaries.
	[Abednego shakes the bowl and drinks up. He returns the bowl to Ojongo, wiping his lips with the back of his hand]

Abednego:	Funny that married or not, I never think of any woman as a she-goat. But this world is one big hunting ground of pining females who find you before you seek them. Let the married ones be warned to keep out of my royal sight: the raking eyes of a he-lion cannot stop themselves from the inviting behinds of ready antelopes.
Ojongo:	What if there are more than one he-lion in the forest . . .
Abednego:	It is not the roar that makes a lion but the lurking thunder in his being. A lion who submits himself to the common curfew is no different from the orphan rabbit on the bush path or the everyday worm that crawls out of the woodwork. I seek my destiny, Ojongo, and it is not for my selfish interest. There are too many suffering wives among my subjects who deserve to be liberated from undeserving husbands. What I need is power that observes no borders.
Ojongo:	Ojongo knows what to do if . . . .
Abednego:	That is the music I like to hear from you . . . . and I pay without fuss anytime it plays! Ojongo, marriage should not be a jailhouse of deprivations for some entrapped woman to cry away her whole lifetime. Think if it was your own daughter!
Ojongo:	The return of the paid dowry is always an option . . .
Abednego:	Why must it be divorce, Ojongo? Or remarriage and all such other boring yawn of custom? Should a woman die in misery simply because she can't afford to leave her husband's home or drop his name?
Ojongo:	It is a very uncommon charm that you are asking for. It can cost you a whole elephant . . .

Abednego:	I will pay the asking price, Ojongo because this is one matter I feel very passionate about.
Ojongo:	I must know why, how far to push the spirits! There must be a personal side to such a quest or the spirits will resist your pretensions.
Abednego:	Ojongo is indeed a clever man! Well, I admit there is a woman.
Ojongo:	Every man has one nibbler at the tenderest spot of his heart.
Abednego:	This is one nibbler who has defied the years . . . She knows like me that the strong winds of destiny will bring our boats together. What happens when that happens cannot be my fault alone.
Ojongo:	She is no city woman. She must have a name.
Abednego *[flaring up]*:	You are asking needless questions! Give me what I want with no further probe!
Ojongo *[shrugs, cool and smug]*:	If you block enquiry, how can we push the spirits? Ojongo needs to know the special woman in your heart or we cannot draw her stars to shine for you?
Abednego *[resignedly]*:	It is Ugochi, princess of Umuachala . . . . You can see how unhappy she is with the person she calls husband.
Ojongo:	The reason for a fight or the purpose of a feast, what is that to Ojongo? Give Ojongo what he eats, and you yourself will eat what you want.
Abednego:	Name what you eat Ojongo, because I need that woman.
Ojongo:	The spirits are whispering that you need her very strongly.
Abednego:	She is a born princess, the only woman who will make a fitting queen by my side on the throne.

Do you see why I can never give up this throne? Let Akaeze employ more witches to seal it up like a forbidden shrine. It will never scare me away. I have you Ojongo, terrible hawk. Make my rear parts strong.

Ojongo: Ojongo has a request of his own because . . . . when the right hand is washing the left hand, the left hand is washing the right hand in turn.

Abednego: Have I not asked you to name your price?

Ojongo: Great One, the vacant stool of Ajofia is waiting to be filled.

Abednego: Ajofia's stool? Ah . . . . Well, why not? Here's my hand three-fold, the due of the fully titled! Is it not always said that a thief's accomplice is a thief himself? You will be installed right after my coronation.

> [*They execute a chieftaincy handshake—three back-hand steals and a firm, final clasp*]

Ojongo: Now, Ojongo can declare your path clear. Great One, your man whose hand does what his mouth says will guide you straight to throne and fame. It is time for action, Great One!

Abednego: I feel like thunder.

Ojongo: Act like it, Great One. This is the sure moment. I know what I have poured inside you.

Abednego: I can pull down mountains, Ojongo.

Ojongo: The power I fed you will make that old woman feel like a brand new maid. Do her this moment and have your throne.

Abednego [*suddenly deflated*]: Ojongo, the mere mention of that Oyidi'a job turns me cold as dead.

Ojongo: You have to be strong, Great One. The inheritance of a palace goes with ancient things and aged wives.

Abednego: Ceremony is different from what you are asking me to do.

Ojongo: The gods cannot be denied. You insisted on their throne. It is only yours when you subdue that woman like the man you are.

Abednego: This one makes me sick to the bones . . . . I need another bottle of the white man's drink!

[Fade]

Act 3, Scene 2

Empty stage representing the fore-ground of the Umudimkpa palace in the misty half-light of early dawn. Sergeant leads his unarmed squad in a security drill. Baton under his left armpit, he stands at stiff attention facing the four men in their extended-line formation. His head turns left and right with the sharpness of a predatory bird and he calls out orders.

Sergeant:	'Shon! Stand aaat ayiz! 'Shon! *[pauses, inspects, then resumes]* Who are we?
Policemen:	We are police!
Sergeant:	Police power?
Policemen:	*Gorment* power!
Sergeant:	*Gorment* power?
Policemen:	No challenge!
Sergeant *[after a brief pause]:*	Men will report security! Order, one by one! Lance Corp'l first, then Constable Number One and the rest, you follow! Men, one by one, forward march!
	[Lance Corp'l marches up close and salutes, followed one at a time by Constables 1, 2 and 3]
Sergeant:	Lance Corp'l, report security!
Lance Corporal:	Shon sir! Native war. Nine police dead, fifteen natives. Three police missing, twenty-eight natives arrested. All dead bodies have been buried, only body of white man is not buried.

Sergeant:	White man's body, check it every day. Order of King and order of Dio. Is that clear?
Lance Corporal:	Yessah! Oga Sergeant, someone is checking every day!
Sergeant:	Make sure it is every day! Orders are orders! Is that clear?
Lance Corporal:	Yessah!
Sergeant:	White man's body very, important!
Lance Corporal:	Yessah! They say it can never, never spoil . . .
Sergeant:	Yes it cannot spoil. Hezekiah soaked it with a special ointment from Iwobi. No burial until when Dio comes back.
Lance Corporal:	Shon sir! No complain!
Sergeant:	Constable Number One . . . . security!
Constable 1:	Shon sir! Native war report! Natives very angry about burials without funerals! First is two big chiefs, then Oche-ilo-eze, buried like common chicken! People very angry! And they blame king for Oche-ilo-eze! And everywhere you go, the same noise and same trouble. No proper funerals, no proper peace.
Sergeant:	Nonsense in opinion, nonsense in private! Why always like this that natives have no brains? This is Straight of emergency! Therefore, no illegal gatherings! Native funeral, local festival, all other pagan nonsense, it is illegal gathering! Is that clear?
Constable 1:	Shon sir! No complain'.
Sergeant:	Constable Number Two . . . . report security!
Constable 2:	Shon sir! Native war report! Natives very angry about rape and very angry about three native women. They are by force in the palace and they have not returned to their husbands.

Sergeant:	Why the noise? Best home on earth for best women is the King's palace. Order is by king! Better life for native women.
Constable 2:	No complaint sir; but native men are sharpening matchets.
Sergeant:	What can a rat do to an iron pot? Those men have equal opportunity! It is dear wife or dear life!
Lance Corporal:	Very true, Oga Sergeant. The man they called woman and laughed is now called lion when their women are like sheep!
Sergeant:	Constable Number Three . . . . security!
Constable 3:	Shon sir! Native war report! Natives ready to kill because of High Mother and the big chiefs. Very angry everywhere! Very, very angry that it is high disgrace for high people to wait every day for small boy! King is who they call small boy, no respect at all. Many, many curses that he must die and never sit on throne.
Sergeant:	That throne . . . . Many bad things we hear but king is adamant.
Constable 3:	He is their brother; he knows what they know . . . .
Sergeant:	I think he even knows more than they know or . . . .
Constable 1:	But someone should advise him to meet with the elders. They are leaders of their people. Why do we bring them every day, they sit here and they wait, he doesn't want to see them?
Sergeant:	It is your own head alone that your big mouth will put in trouble one day! Parade will dismiss! Dismiss!

[They relax, mill around, chatting. Exeunt one way as Abednego in white toga enters from the opposite end, Ojongo a step behind him]

Ojongo:

I wonder if anyone can ever win a debate with you. Yours is a closet full of stubborn answers.

Abednego:

If I must tell you this, Ojongo ... My life has been a battle from the cradle. A legion of archers, day and night come at me from all angles, shooting blinding questions. I learnt very early to trust in my own answers for survival. I am always ready to match wits with anyone, anytime.

Ojongo:

Then see these ones today. I can help you further with Oyidi'a, put herbs in the fire and fill her nostrils with rare smoke as she sits there. She will become dizzy, easy to pick as a woman.

Abednego:

But Akaeze and his boy, Orimili are still there! If wishes were fire, those two would burn me down from head to toe. I'm only giving them time to burn themselves out. When they have become cold as ash, I will sit down with them.

Ojongo:

If you wish today, Great One, I have something in my goatskin bag to turn them to the coldest ash for you. Who on this earth can be fire in your face with that power in your hand?

Abednego:

Let me see it!

[Ojongo rushes off-stage]

Abednego *[aside]*:

The big moment is here .... when the scorpion, *akpi* must prove that he is the kid terror that fears no size of seat or buttocks. The whole nation should get set for the sting of *Odogwu Ozala*, the mighty one of the scrubland!

[Fade]

ACT 3, SCENE 3

Throne Room of Umudimkpa, the throne hooded in black being the solitary item on the dais. Akaeze and Oyidi'a are sitting tiredly on one of the benches in the hall, their backs leaned against the side wall. Both are dozing, a flute playing intermittently in the background.

[Enter Orimili Obiora]

Akaeze:	Ah, Orimili! You kept us fidgeting . . . . We feared the very worst.
Orimili Obiora:	Father Akaeze and Mother Oyidi'a, please accept my greetings and my deepest apologies for lateness. *[He sits]*
Oyidia:	It is so unusual of you to keep us waiting. We were here and not here, our eyes stuck on the endless road of anxiety.
Orimili Obiora:	I am indeed sorry, Oyidi'a but it is this woman again.
Oyidi'a:	Your wife, Ugochi?
Orimili Obiora:	Who else will kill me?
Oyidi'a:	What is it again this time, Orimili?
Orimili Obiora:	High Mother, must a man be heard groaning or grunting all the time? Let's just mind the affairs of Umudimkpa.
Oyidi'a:	No matter should take precedence over your home, Orimili Obiora. Akaeze and I are already on the way out like Oche-ilo-eze, and you are the last beacon. You must be standing very well

because a man whose home is reeling in the wind cannot shoulder the peace of a whole kingdom.

Orimili Obiora: Oyidi'a, the ache in my heart is private, sorry . . . . The business of the kingdom will take no second place.

Oyidi'a: This is the sorry pit you find in the life of great figures, why the blind side of their lives is often such a pain to observe: they burn out themselves to light up the whole world but leave their own homes in smoke and ruins. You will not travel that route, Orimili Obiora, not when I am still alive and have counsel in my tongue. Our father Akaeze will spare me a little time to hear you out before we talk Umudimkpa.

Orimili Obiora: Ugochi is demanding proof of manhood from me. That's it!

Oyidi'a: What is the meaning of that one?

Orimili Obiora: She is . . . a princess, daughter of a king (how did I ever forget?) . . . and she suffered an outrage of indignities the other night . . . . She feels reduced to nothing in the eyes of the whole world . . . . and where is her husband? (that is the question she's been shouting in my ears!) I must be a man and do something; otherwise, I don't deserve to be called her husband ever again!

Oyidi'a: All of us were humiliated, and it was beyond words! But how is that your fault? What does Ugochi expect from you?

Orimili Obiora: She says there is no real man left in Umudimkpa. I've asked her to go back to Umuachala and never come back!

Akaeze: It is a bad time for harsh words, Orimili.

Orimili Obiora: The woman is driving me mad! What name did she not call me this morning? I am not fit to speak as a man except I go with a matchet and bring her the head of you know who.

Oyidi'a *[with a deep grunt]:*   I know her pain as a woman . . . . Ugochi is not the bad girl that her occasional outbursts make her seem.

> *[Lights dim. Glimpses of Ugochi and her daughter, Adaobi busy with domestic chores in the darkened corner . . . . They set down a mortar, business-like; Ugochi fetches two long pestles and hands one to Adaobi. They stand pounding grain and chatting]*

Ugochi: I can never understand your father and his people! Sometimes, I think my marriage to him was a bad mistake!

Adaobi: Mother, I don't like this thing you often say!

Ugochi: Shut up your mouth! You are always siding with him. See how they allow a bastard who should be rotting in prison to be the one shoving us ourselves into prison. Is it not better to die?

Adaobi: My father will always think very well before he does something.

Ugochi: Think very well, is it? Your father thinks things to death, that man! I should have left that slave girl for him.

Adaobi: Ajachi again?

Ugochi: Who else but her? I did not suspect his motive at the time; but I do now. He insisted so strongly that I spare her life. Maybe he too had eyes on her.

Adaobi: Ajachi was your slave girl and when she became pregnant, you plucked out her two eyes and threw her into the evil forest. I've heard you a dozen times on that story.

Ugochi:	Because it is the root of my trouble with your father who likes to be tender-hearted like *osukwu* palm-fruit! He never forgave me when he found out after our marriage. Yet I don't understand his problem. Ajachi was my own slave and nobody's business what I chose to do to her!

[She pounds furiously; Adaobi stops]

Adaobi:	It is ready, I think.

[Ugochi scoops a fistful and examines it. Without a word they bend and together lug the mortar away from stage as lights brighten]

Oyidi'a *[stretches, yawning tiredly]:*   Ugochi, my eagle . . . . I must speak to her again . . . . An excessive pride in father is a killer disease if it makes a woman headstrong in her husband's home.

Akaeze:	See how we are diverting! We are leaving the biggest hunt of our life to chase after houseflies.
Orimili Obiora:	Pardon my retreat, Akaeze. I never really wanted to bare my private heartaches. Every man should bear his own with character.
Oyidi'a:	Orimili Obiora, you will not behead anybody, neither will you lose your own head at this awkward time. You must be standing firm to lead our people for us. It is your destiny.
Akaeze:	For me, the race is over . . .
Oyidi'a:	Please don't speak those words, Akaeze.
Akaeze:	Oyidi'a, the drums of death are already beating in my ears. I hear the footsteps and I am in step with Oche-ilo-eze.
Oyidi'a:	Are we to yield space to this rascal when the kingdom is upside down as it is? He can't wait to dance on our graves . . . . and he has enough madness to pull down all landmarks.

Akaeze:	Oyidi'a, landmark has a new meaning to me . . . . You and I were dozing here a short while ago . . . . but mine was not just an ordinary nap . . . . I'd gone into a deep trance . . . . Ogbuefi Iwobi sat on a high stool right there with his children around him . . .

[Soft melody on 'ichaka' as lights dim. Enter silhouettes of Iwobi, his four sons, his daughter Uzoma and Hezekiah the interpreter in a mimed dance. The boys set up a high stool for their father whilst Hezekiah relieves the girl of the pan she is carrying on her head. The children dance a few more steps and squat on the floor around the stool, the four boys holding the legs of the stool as their father mounts it, a big bible in hand.]

Akaeze *[continuing]*:	I was saying something to Ogbuefi but he did not care to listen. He opened the white man's big book on his lap and to my greatest surprise, he began to read it like he was the one who wrote the words . . . . *[Iwobi opens the bible on his laps and pores over the pages]*.
Akaeze *[continuing]*:	His words are still echoing in my ears.
Ogbuefi Iwobi:	Let every man receive this message like me. We all shall become sons of God and overcome all the battles of life; we shall no more call on the dead to come and fight for us. This is a choice every man must make for himself in his lifetime. I have chosen for myself and my household.
Akaeze *[continuing]*:	The other interpreter then came forward (remember that skinny one that wept for his dead master?) He began to teach Iwobi's children the white man's language.

[Iwobi's children squatting on the floor at the feet of his stool, make a lively class with their rhythmic clapping and chorusing. Their teacher,

Hezekiah standing before them, gyrates and demonstrates as he teaches]

Hezekiah/Chorus *(line by line):* A man!
A pan!
A man and a pan!
A pan and a man!
This is a man!
This is a pan!
Is this a man?
Yes, it is a man!
Is this a pan?
Yes, it is a pan!

[With increasing intensity the chant and its clapping accompaniment are repeated, the class rising to dance with its teacher in a single file. Iwobi gets down from his high stool and joins the dance at the rear, his bible held aloft. Exeunt all, along with stool, pan and other items]

Akaeze *[concluding]:* Something tells me that this is the most important landmark that we ought to build fast for our children.

Orimili Obiora: That is exactly the words of Oche-ilo-eze, his very last gasp, that power to understand the white man's written things would be the strongest amulet in the new world . . . .

Akaeze: It is a great weapon, obviously, but in wrong hands here; a villain is using it to beat us on the head like baby rats!

Oyidi'a: He killed Oche-ilo-eze. Who is next?

Orimili Obiora: My worst fear that night was for you, High Mother, standing all through with us in that airless coop, how you and Akaeze could see daybreak.

Oyidi'a: The pain in my heart that night only spoke strength to my body. Everything was darkness though . . . . I thought I was dead.

Akaeze:	I came out of that grave with only one resolve, alive or dead, to never speak to that beast again . . . . Sadly, we must break the silence now or posterity will not forgive us.
Orimili Obiora:	If we don't talk, the killings will not stop . . .
Oyidi'a:	But how can we reason with a madman and not sound like we are the ones with trouble in the head?
Akaeze:	Orimili will be our sole mouthpiece for the whole kingdom. It is a fitting match as both of them are age mates.
Orimili Obiora:	A huge burden, father Akaeze . . . . but you have not mentored me in vain.
Akaeze:	The timeless wisdom of our forefathers will shape your words. A rabbit that dances on a bush path hears a drumming which no one else can hear.

[Ebili dashes in]

Ebili:	*Nna Anyi* Akaeze! The lass Akweke has been seized again! I saw that bully they call Sajent and two men . . . . They covered her mouth like this and carried her through the small back door.
Oyidi'a:	But . . . . Akaeze, didn't that boy swear to us just an eye-blink ago? The girl took shelter with us but he came over begging that we release her in peace to go back to her father's house!
Akaeze:	Did you hear me utter a single word? I knew he was lying.
Oyidi'a:	I'm ashamed to have been deceived by him again!
Orimili Obiora:	Apiti has words to sell common spittle as a full river . . . . We were childhood playmates. The only truth in his mouth is the next lie

Ebili:	*Nna anyi* Akaeze, I sense a sudden desperation. Apiti will kill the story in that girl's mouth. Akweke is in great danger.
Oyidi'a:	Not as the House of Ajofia knows how to protect its own. Even in ashes, it is still nobody's playground!
Akaeze:	The wayward may eat without inquiry to die without notice!

[Lights dim in the gloomy silence. Ebili sits near Orimili and plays on his flute, Oyidia taking up the song. All join]

Oyidi'a/Chorus *[alternating]*:

Akweke olima, Akw'eke olima
Dooh olimaima, dooh olima
Akweke olima, Akw'eke olima
Dooh olimaima, dooh olima

[Lance Corporal bursts in]

Lance Corporal *[shouting]*:   Order! The king says stop that song!

[Thoroughly ignored, Lance Corporal gets nervous and excited, shakes his truncheon threateningly at the singers]

Oyidi'a/Chorus *[unrelenting]*:

Akw'eke m'debelu n'onwo n'ozurozi
Dooh olimaima dooh olima
Akw'eke m'debelu n'onwo n'ozurozi
Dooh olimaima dooh olima
Akweke olima, Akw'eke olima
Dooh olimaima, dooh olima

[Lance Corporal is all worked up]

Lance Corporal *[shouting]*:   Stop it! Stop it! Don't tempt me! Don't make me break your old heads! Stop! Orders are orders!

[Fade]

Act 3, Scene 4

Throne room at Umudimkpa, the throne still hooded in black and a rickety table with two straight-backed wooden chairs the only furniture on the dais. On the floor in the hall, a line of wooden benches rings the side walls.

> *[Enter Lance Corporal and Constable 3, looking flushed and combative. They exchange a high-five]*

Constable 3: This job is power! *Gorment* power, no challenge!

Lance Corporal: We can finish anybody! Who *born* dog?

Constable 3: High this or high that, their eyes have seen pepper now, now!

Lance Corporal: We finished them, tied them with ropes and locked them up!

Constable 3: Orders are orders! No shaking!

> *[Exeunt Lance Corporal & Constable 3. Enter Abednego and Ojongo from the chamber side]*

Abednego *[drinks from a bottle of gin in hand]*: Nobody is above the law!

Ojongo: You are the hunter; you know what you want! This is your best moment. Make the big move.

Abednego: I am confident that Ugochi will come, Ojongo. The moment she hears that Obiora is back in detention, you will see her here. I want that woman like a man has never wanted a woman.

Ojongo: Great One, the throne is talking of Oyidi'a, not Ugochi! All my preparation is for Oyidi'a and

	she is ready . . . . *[furtive whisper]* I filled her lungs with smoke as I promised. She is ready for you.
Abednego *[flustered]*:	But I've told you that I'm not ready for her . . . . . . To tell you the truth, I don't know if I can ever be ready for that thing . . . .
Ojongo:	Do you want this throne or not? Everything is set for you. Meet their man, mate their woman. Which one first?

[Enter five palace belles, running with delighted shrieks and squeals to mob Abednego]

Abednego:	Pretty ones! Pretty ones!
Belles *[preening]*:	We are more than pretty! We are be-a-u-ti-ful!
Abednego:	Hey, you are interrupting a very important matter of state.
Belles:	Are we not important?
Abednego *[moves to free himself from the cluster]*:	You are more than important . . . . but playtime is later. You must leave, for now!
Belles:	Awhhhhh!
Abednego:	Don't worry your pretty heads. I know what you want.
Belles:	No you don't!

[Enter Lance Corporal and 2, lugging Rev Jones' big box]

Lance Corporal:	Shon sir! We arrested it. Orders are orders!
Abednego:	Ahaaa! The white preacher's box that didn't go to heaven with him! I am the right man on earth to keep it for him. Move it to that corner. Very good, very good!

[Constables comply, then stand back, grinning sheepishly as the belles flock around Abednego]

Lance Corporal *[salutes]*: Awaiting orders, king, sir!

Abednego: What orders again? You have brought what I want, finish! Go! I will check everything by myself because I know the contents.

[Exeunt Lance Corporal and Constable 3]

Abednego: Sweethearts, you too must leave. But never mind. I know what you want.

Belles: No you don't

Abednego: Come on, I'm the man who knows what every woman wants and always gives it. You will get it, I promise but not now.

Belles: Awhhhhh! Why not now?

Abednego: Come on, girls, you can't expect your honeycomb everywhere and everytime. Hey, what are we talking about?

[The belles in unison point at the box]

Abednego *[surprised, disappointed]:* Aw, the box? You want . . . . presents, only presents? Well, if that is all you want, no matter! I'll give you something you all love so much! Mirrors! Mirrors!

Belles *[swooning]:* Ooooh . . . . Mirrors!

Abednego: Yes, mirrors for you all! Now, off you go. Come back later!

[Exeunt four belles clapping and whooping. The last one sidles awhile with Ojongo, whispering intently]

Belle: You said he is going to pick me as his special one . . . .

Ojongo: Do what I asked you to do.

Belle: I am doing it . . . but it is not working . . . He doesn't even notice me.

Ojongo: You are too hasty. Be patient.

Belle:	I shan't be patient if I lose out.
Ojongo:	Then a bitch becomes a witch.
Belle:	Guess who will be her first victim.
Ojongo:	Only a foolish she-dog. The one thinking to stop the rushing waves by barking at the angry sea!
Abednego:	What are you whispering with that one?
Ojongo:	She is threatening to kill Ojongo if anything happens to the love of her life!
Abednego:	Is that me . . . or someone else?
Belle:	Who else but you?
Abednego:	Great. What's your own name?
Belle:	Iquo . . . . you keep forgetting . . .
Abednego:	Never mind, Iquo. Hmm, Iquo, Iquo! We shall equalize soon, again . . . . Equality! All right, run off . . . Come back later.

[Exit Iquo with a languorous catwalk]

Ojongo:	You don't even remember pet names?
Abednego:	The taste of bush meat is when you chew it, not what you call it
Ojongo:	Iquo is crying day and night . . . She is dying of love for you.
Abednego:	Love . . . . the magic word by which the brainless are put under a spell and taken captive! Any man who believes that word in the mouth of a woman has joined the living dead!
Ojongo:	You sound like you have no faith in love and women!
Abednego:	Ojongo, I enjoy loads of attention from all sorts of women! But I will never be fooled by their common use of empty words. Love is the cheap

	song of all pretenders . . . . Now, don't give me that wounded-rabbit look . . . . I am not saying what you don't know already: Most women out there would marry monkeys if money grew on trees!
Ojongo:	You are a hard man, Great One.
Abednego:	Not harder than you with fifteen wives, Ojongo.
Ojongo:	A dozen bitter hens are not chasing after me with paternity claims for their brood. Doesn't that say something to you?
Abednego:	The wind cannot be bothered by a song it left behind! I don't care what desperate cackles are tumbling at my heels. All life is a roll, and all sorts of claims chase after successful men like me. Nobody would claim me if I was nobody!
Ojongo:	Your coronation is coming . . . . best moment to gather your past and present into one tidy family story.
Abednego:	It is a better opportunity to begin a new story which I must tell in my own way. Did anybody in Umudimkpa ever think this day would come? Did man or woman guess that I would be back in their face to become king and rule over them? I am the easy food they all spat out of their dirty mouths . . . . Now, every one of them will beg for crumbs off me!
Ojongo:	Are you ready to meet Akaeze then?
Abednego:	I think the time has come to face him and his little gang. It is going to be a debate to end all debates! Bring them! But ah! No! That can wait. Ugochi is here! Everything else must wait.

[Enter Ugochi, charged and very upset]

Ugochi *[spitting at Ojongo]*:	You are the one they call Ojongo! *Tufia!* Shameless drummer that drums for the shameless dancer!

Ojongo [restraining himself with evident difficulty]:   Ojongo   will
step back, but only in wisdom . . . . Chei! A man
meets his own compound hen at dawn and she
has grown biting teeth overnight!

Abednego: Let me handle this, Ojongo. Didn't I tell you she
would come?

[Exit Ojongo, burning and bristling]

Ugochi: So it was bait in your plot? Detention of my
husband to force my feet into the palace!

Abednego: Your husband broke the law. Nobody is above
the law.

Ugochi: Which law? Which useless law?

Abednego: Ugochi, you were born to rule. So begin to think
of your future, not the past. Your future is in this
palace.

Ugochi: Apiti, may diarrhea that has neither mother nor
father empty your insides; and may it dump
your bones in the evil forest!

Abednego: Ugochi, speak like the princess you are and the
queen I am trying to make you. You can't spend
the rest of your life in the shadow of a previous
mistake.

Ugochi [livid, stamps her feet in rage and turns away, hissing riotously]:
Beast! Brute!

Abednego: Those are terms of endearment that lovers may
spray or spare themselves! But think what you
are missing—all daytime by the king's side; all
bedtime with a real man! Real man, Ugochi!

Ugochi [in evident exasperation]: Apiti, where is my husband?

Abednego [half amused, idles, then drifts closer]:   Forget that boy, Ugochi.
Forget him, my queen. You and I are made for
each other. I am the man you need in your life!

Ugochi [backtracks as Abednego presses closer]:   Don't you dare touch me! Don't ever! [panics] What is . . . . ? Apiti! [screams] Apiti!

Abednego [freezes suddenly and shrugs]: I can wait . . . . I know the woman in you wants to be rushed but . . . you still . . . need some time to come around! It's just a woman thing.

Ugochi: You disgusting bastard!

Abednego: I said we shall agree our terms of endearment. Call me anything that turns you on.

> [Ugochi huffs and puffs, then storms out. Abednego laughs, drinks gin from his bottle. Ojongo re-enters]

Abednego: That is the woman for me, Ojongo.

Ojongo [in exasperation]: Oyidi'a is ready for you, Great One.

Abednego: It's like all women want a piece of me, those with names and those without names too.

Ojongo: Is it a thing of rejoicing? To be torn in pieces by costumed dogs alias Pimpim-Sinsim . . . . or slaughtered and quartered by enraged husbands? Great One, the throne's call for you is Oyidi'a; your answer must be now or never.

Abednego: No, not now. Not ever! If I can't catch the fire to forget myself and do the bad job, what next? See, I drink . . . I must drink white man's gin. I need the fire! [takes a long nervous swig at his bottle and sighs in relief] Look, I want this throne with every bit of me; but the Oyidi'a thing is awful. Prepare me for the big talk with Akaeze and his leftovers! The Oyidi'a matter later!

Ojongo: I will fetch you the amulet of power from my goatskin bag.

> [Exit Ojongo, chamber side]

Abednego *[aside]:* White man's gin! Wicked fire! Burns all the way down throat and stomach to where the lion lives. I can't touch Oyidi'a . . . . But any other woman now is in trouble! Any woman!

[Lights dim as a soft singing of "Akweke olima" floats in. Abednego casts about nervously]

Abednego *[shouts]:* Ojongo! Ojongo!

[Ojongo dashes in and the singing stops]

Ojongo: What is it? What is it?

Abednego: A strange voice was singing. I heard it . . . .

Ojongo *[in near-exasperation]:* Great One, you are no stranger to the wicked tricks of rascally spirits. I'm on a powerful incantation over a special amulet for you. Would you let them distract us?

Abednego: All right, just go ahead. I'll sit here and wait.

[Exit Ojongo. Abednego, bottle in hand, sits on a bench in the corner, a trite nervous and shifty; he drinks from time to time. Lights brighten, dim again. Suddenly, the singing returns; Abednego jumps up startled, stepping backward in terror. The singing goes on and off, the unseen singer seeming to shift base from one side to the other like a ghost in the walls. Backing away, he feels a tap on his shoulder and turns quickly. Akweke is standing there]

Abednego *[shaking with fear]:* You again! You-u-u-u!

Akweke: Where is your great manhood? You still want something?

Abednego: Keep away from me! Keep away!

Akweke: Tell your men to release me . . . Let me go my way before dusk returns. The wailing python shall visit in search of her missing egg! You don't know a python until you find her in your bed!

Abednego:	Ojongo!

[Abednego turns and flees into his bedchamber. Blackout on stage. The light returns dim as Abednego re-emerges with Ojongo. No trace of Akweke]

Abednego *[shaking with fear]*: She was here just now! Believe me, she was here!

Ojongo: But there is no sign of anybody.

Abednego: I tell you, she was here! She even spoke to me!

Ojongo *[scowls in disbelief, hisses deeply]*: I warned you to let go of that girl.

Abednego: Ojongo, I will not live in fear of a small girl that has not even formed her full breasts!

Ojongo: That one's age is not what you see. She is a spirit without years, betrothed to a he-lion.

Abednego: I have conquered she-lions and female dragons in the past. What makes this one different?

Ojongo: Ojongo knows what to do . . . .

Abednego: Don't wait for me to ask for everything. Do something and be paid your bloody price.

[Ojongo quickly stuffs four small earthen bowls, with grasses and setting them in the four corners, lights them up with a burning taper]

Ojongo: Ojongo has herbs and spices to attract or repel every tribe of spirits! Be these ones from the hills or they dwell in the depth of valleys, fires in my chosen bowls, speak in smoke, speak in incense! Flush out the invaders . . . . Send them away!

[The palace fills up with smoke. Lights dim.]

Ojongo: Choi! Choi!

[Fade]

ACT 3, SCENE 5

Throne room at Umudimkpa palace, the throne still hooded in black on the dais. Abenego is seated on a cane chair at a wooden table backing the throne, puffing self-importantly on his pipe. Enter three brightly costumed belles, each holding a large ceremonial fan made of a cowhide circular sheet ringed with bright ostrich feathers. They pose with panache, position themselves flirtatiously around King Abednego and proceed to fan him stylishly]

Abednego:	Take note, girls, take note. Which hand is fanning with love and which hand is fanning for fanning sake. The king can see everyone without turning his head.
Zizzi:	My hand is love, O king. I love my king dearly.
Pimpim:	My love has the tenderness of silk. You feel it for ever.
Iquo:	Love pure as gold, my gift to my precious king.
Abednego:	No more noises! Let only your hands do all the talking.
	[Enter Ojongo; thrusts a cow horn into Abednego's hand]
Ojongo:	Hold this in your left hand as you speak to Akaeze and gang. From time to time, you bring it close to your mouth like this. I will sit in hiding to catch every bullet aimed at you.
Abednego:	Why won't you be by my side?
Ojongo:	Ojongo can shock his foes without showing face or hand! The power in that horn is ten Ojongo!

Abednego:	Proof is waiting in the arena. Tell the guards to bring the gang!

[Exit Ojongo. Abednego leans back in his chair, puffing at his pipe and tapping his feet as Ekwe chant breaks out]

Ekwe Chant:	Olue oge mmanwu ji agba egwu

    (It's dancing time for masquerades)
Ejeyamma!
    (Tralala!)
Olue oge mmanwu ga agba egwu
    (It's dancing time for masquerades)
Ejeyamma!
    (Tralala!)
Olue oge mmanwu ga agba egwu
    (It's dancing time for masquerades)
Ejeyamma mma, mma mma mma, Ejeyamma!
    (Tralala lala! Tralala!)

[Enter Sergeant leading Akaeze, Oyidi'a, Orimili Obiora and Ebili in single file, Lance Corporal in the rear. The captive four stands before him, hands tied at the wrists, faces expressionless. Abednego, deep in talk and laughing with the girl behind his chair, pretends not to notice their presence even after Sergeant signals it by clearing his throat rather noisily]

Sergeant:	Your Highness, King and Paramount Ruler of all Umudimkpa, greetings from your loyal subjects. Long may you live!

[Abednego turns, sees the ropes on Akaeze and Oyidi'a and jumps to his feet in mock horror]

Abednego:	Sergeant! What is this? Who roped these chiefs of the kingdom like common goats?
Sergeant:	Your Highness, these ones are rebels! They sang the forbidden song and were caught red-handed!

Abednego:	Sergeant! Are you mad? How dare you permit a rope on these great people? The pride and glory of this kingdom, in ropes! This is a blow to my fatherland. No patriot like me will take this! Somebody will pay dearly!
Sergeant:	Your Highness, I can explain.
Abednego:	Don't explain that rubbish about orders from above. I don't care what the white man told you to do here!
Sergeant:	Shon sir! Sorry sir!
Abednego:	White man has father and mother in his own country! Untie my own people immediately!
Sergeant:	Shon sir! King sir! Lance Corp'l, obey the last order!

[The four are quickly untied by the two policemen]

Abednego *[snapping his fingers at his female attendants]*: Pretty   ones, you too, out! Leave me for now. I'm not happy anymore.

[Exeunt the three belles. Abednego paces]

Sergeant:	King sir . . . .
Abednego:	Don't talk to me, Sergeant. You have caused me enough trouble. Go away with your Corp'l and leave me alone. Only the guards can stay because they are the only ones who know respect for good people. My people must be respected!

[Enter the three constables. They flank Abednego, stroking their batons]

Sergeant:	Shon sir!
Lance Corporal:	King Sir!

[Sergeant marches off, Lance Corporal following]

Abednego:	Please take your seats, father Akaeze and mother Oyidi'a. This should be a family talk. I am still your son.

[Akaeze and Oyidi'a sit woodenly. Orimili Obiora and Ebili remain standing. Abednego sits.]

Abednego:	It is one blood and one family; never mind that the white man has made me your king and calls you my subjects. I feel very bad that Orimili Obiora has allowed strangers in our midst to mistreat you behind my back. If there was a better sense of duty in his head, he should have brought matters to my notice; then nobody suffers any harassment at all from those aliens. You are my own people. I insist on full respect for Akaeze and Oyidi'a, full respect! Even if Orimili Obiora and I have our own disagreement as age mates, these two very special people are still our father and mother; and they deserve our greatest respect. I insist!

[Orimili Obiora sits down away from the elderly pair]

Orimili Obiora:	You have spoken as a brother; so I must respond as one. Our father and mother here are too old for this type of stress, like what they endured the other night. They should be allowed to retire home and rest. The three of us here can discuss as siblings and age mates for the good of the land.
Abednego:	You forget that the white man's anger is still very hot! You cannot blame him as his brother was killed in this very palace. That is the big problem facing me and you. The kingdom can start burning if any of us is thinking of sleep.
Ebili:	I am not thinking of sleep at all. I want my flute back. One of your men seized it. The one they call Kopul.

Abednego:

I really wonder why this one of all people should be part of this discussion!

Orimili Obiora:

Is he not our brother? This is family.

Abednego:

You forget again the big problem on our head: the white man's beloved brother was killed right here by Egbuna, our very own kinsman. It is a kind of crime that the white man calls a name much bigger than abomination! If that did not happen, slave or cockroach could join us and talk. I am a democrat to the core!

Orimili Obiora:

As one democrat to the other, should our talk be mere words of mouth? Shouldn't we listen to each other's heart beat too? The land we love so dearly must not burn to ashes before our eyes.

Abednego:

My detractors are bigots who hate their own fatherland. Little blind rodents, vermin of sabotage, demons of discord! All they want is to pull down at all costs. They are full of hate, prejudice and bile, maligning the best even before a test.

Orimili Obiora:

Your fight with them should not turn against the whole country. Nobody can win a battle for hearts with crazy gunshots and blind strokes of the matchet. Our people don't deserve the present siege.

Abednego:

A white man was killed! Where is Egbuna, the killer?

Orimili Obiora:

Your men should tell us because he was still in their custody when he was last seen in public. The indiscriminate torture of innocent bystanders cannot produce a wanted fugitive . . .

Abednego [*rising threateningly*]: I have refused to be provoked to any reaction. But the insolence of my detractors is hitting the sky in the face. Does anyone of you really know what I am today? Do you wish to try the power of the white man that is now in my hands? I decided to see you face to face to give this final warning. The present provocation must stop because it will no longer be tolerated. But if anyone prefers a little display, the kingdom will be served a few knocks in the right places for a little more sanity.

Orimili Obiora *[unruffled]*: Whose interest is served by a rage of fists and batons? A strong man who tests his strength by punching his own mother may not be called a fool to his face; but the grave he must dig would mock him for life.

Abednego: I am humbled by the trust of our illustrious forefathers. That, in their great wisdom, the resting patriarchs broke their solemn sleep of ages to choose me as your saviour is clear to even a blind man. Umudimkpa needs a saviour because these are perilous times. In the long history of our great nation, there has never been such a desperate need for somebody who knows book, to rule the kingdom. Umudimkpa should thank their stars that I am a son of the soil, the only one who knows what the white man knows. I hear his talk when he speaks and I read his magic when he writes it. I am the only one upon this earth who can appease his anger unless there is someone who prefers Umuachala to repeat here!

Orimili Obiora: Our people deserve their freedom to live and die by their own values. Tell the white man for us that this land is hard on any invader. Umudimkpa is never late to battle.

Abednego *[regains his seat]*: You are forgetting again. Why do you forget? It is not invader we are talking about; not invader but spirit! White man is a spirit! Nobody could fight him when he was still quiet and far, far away. Is it now that he is here with us and his anger is burning that anyone can make *fim*? Let me know who can face white man in this land if not me.

Ebili: Return my flute and see if I will not blow our hearts into the white man's ears. He will hear without words that the land is mourning . . . He will hear of rapes . . . abductions . . . murders . . . chaos and corpses . . . and sudden graves . . . He will hear much more of the evil that has been happening in the last few days . . .

Abednego *[relights his pipe and puffs heavily]*: If his brother was spared by death, the white man's mood might be different, possibly even open to flutes and dances. But he is full of grief and anger this moment (who can blame him?) He wants to bury his brother by himself; but an emergency has rushed him back to Ubulu. We are waiting for his return.

Ebili: Umudimkpa will honour that burial because that man was a friend. My flute shall sing his tribute up to the sky.

Abednego: That is not the way of the white people. He will be buried quietly, what they call dust to dust. But never mind, you will have your flute at my coronation to blow your head off, since that is your life's greatest ambition.

[Re-enter Sergeant breathlessly]

Sergeant *[much agitated]*: Your Highness! Your Highness! These people should be hanged! All hanged!

Abednego: Sergeant, what kind of madness carries you this way into my royal presence?

Sergeant: Your Highness, this country is evil . . . . and these ones sitting here are not human beings! They have done a terrible wicked thing.

Abednego: Sergeant, what do you mean?

Sergeant: King, the body of the white man! These animals have gone there and stolen it! The white man's body is gone, King! Disappeared!

[Pandemonium . . . . Fade]

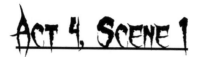

ACT 4, SCENE 1

The king's public square at Umudimkpa. Black-out on stage as a loud wailing is heard, followed by yells, frightened screams and deep groans. The thick darkness lightens a little, revealing in silhouettes a mass of people in various postures, some keening, others grunting or gnashing their teeth or just moping. Sergeant and the three constables are standing like frozen statues at various points, looking grim and stern, big vicious batons in their clenched fists. Ebili narrates from a seated position amongst the audience.

Ebili: What followed were two days of fury and madness. A frenzy of brutality was unleashed on our people . . . . Terror like a rage of foul spirits . . . . Everywhere you turned, someone was getting the beating of his life. They marched in murderous rage, house to house, lane by lane. My people, words fail me to tell you all . . . .

                [Half light on stage. Instant animation, Sergeant and his men raiding and beating up the masses]

Policemen: Where is the body of the white man? Where is the body of the white man?

Ebili: Blinding allegations were spat into our eyes. Accusations upon accusations! Some of you were even roped into their fiction . . . . They said you were part of a plot to undermine their king! You took beatings for something you knew nothing about.

Sergeant: We know your plot, you blinkers! You aim for king to think us unreliable . . . . then we lose our jobs?

Policemen *[beating people]:*   Ahhh! We shall kill you first! Kill all of you!

Sergeant: Because of you useless people, the king's coronation has been postponed. Postponed because of you!

Policemen *[beating the people]:*   Because of you! Because of you!

[Sergeant blows his whistle; his men crowd him hastily]

Sergeant: Attention! We have just received top secret information!

Policemen *[frozen attention]:*   I swear on my honour to keep a secret secret!

Sergeant: It is from usually reliable sources . . . .

Policemen: It is my duty to hear every secret! I must hear!

Sergeant *[furtively]:*   This is a special secret. It is very special.

Policemen: I swear on my honour to keep a secret secret!

Sergeant *[hushed tone]:*   Hear it in your ears. We now know the truth . . . . The natives used the white man's body to make a big juju!

Policemen: Arrghhhhh!

Constable 3:   That is not the full story!

Policemen *[frozen attention]:*   I swear on my honour to keep a secret secret!

Constable 3:   The natives ate the white man's body as meat for strong juju!

Policemen: Arrrrghhhhhh!

Sergeant: Terrible!! The terrible evil of man eaters! They eat a fellow man so the power in his spirit will enter their body!

Constable 3:   Sarge, wait! These foolish natives, they now have the power of white man himself?

Sergeant: Then they finish us! They finish me and you!

Constable 3: No! We kill them first!

Policemen *[beating people]:* You ate the man! You ate the man! Where is the body? Where is the body of the white man?

Ebili: The people had no voice at first . . . compounds were raided, men and women brutalized . . . . even children were not spared.

Grieving woman *[stepping forward with a little child]:* See my four-year old son, beaten into stupor. Does he know a white man?

Constable 3: Shut up, silly woman! One more '*fim*' from your lips, you die!

Ebili: People took the beatings in turns . . . each man nursed his pains in quietude and cursed his stars in private . . . everybody was suffering; but silence covered the land.

Policemen *[beating more people]:* Where is the body of the white man? Where is the body of the white man?

Ebili: But the pains and grief of a captive people always scream to sunlight in the end . . . Hear me, good people, tyranny is like brigandage, a reign of terror like a night of darkness, a monster that creeps upon a people to seize their neck in a vice grip; but tyranny is never for ever . . . . for tyrants are only as strong as the silence of their people. The end of tyranny is the dawn of voices, a word here, a question there . . . . a cry that dares to cry out becomes an outcry . . . . the bully melts and justice rejoices in the open fields. That is Umudimkpa since this afternoon when our battered people began to find their voices . . . You can hear them yourselves, in seeming platitudes . . . .

People:	Look over there! Look over there! The earth is soft and red!It is like a new digging! There, yes, there, that one! It may be the grave . . . . It has to be the grave!

[Policemen quickly source digging implements]

Sergeant:	Dig!

[Four men strip instantly and begin to dig. The constables sing and clap hands in rhythm with the swing of implements]

Constables:	Lebra, toro-toro (Labourer, three-penny hire) A day! Lebra, toro-toro (Labourer, three—penny hire) A day! !

Men:	There is nothing!
Sergeant:	Nothing again? So, where is the body of the white man?

Policemen *[beating the people]:* Where is the body of the white man? Where is the body of the white man?

Ebili:	Pain can kill many things. I've seen pain crash walls of iron and break a will of steel . . . . But pain is powerless against humour, for pained humour is the deadly fang of hounded lambs.

Sergeant *[sternly]:*	We shall ask you the question this one last time!
Policemen:	Where is the body of the white man?
People:	The body of the white man?
Policemen:	Yes, the body of the white man! Where is it?
Somebody:	It is on the bones of the white man!
People:	Yes, on his bones, on his bones! On his bones! On his bones!

Sergeant:	Order! What nonsense? Who's turning this matter into a joke?
Somebody:	Who is turning white man into a joke?
People *[to one another]*:	Who is turning a joke into white man!
Sergeant:	Shut up, all of you! Shut up!
People *[to one another]*:	Who can shut up the white man? Can you shut up the white man? Who can shut up the white man? Can you shut . . . .
Sergeant *[beside himself]*:	Don't mess with me! Don't you dare mess with me!
People *[to one another, bleating like sheep]*:	M - e - e - s s ? M-e-e-e-e-ss!
Sergeant:	All right! You want to turn to goats, do you?
People:	M-e-e-e-e-ss!
Sergeant:	I will beat you like goats! Beat you silly, like silly goats!
People:	M-e-e-e-e-e-e-ess!
	[Sergeant leads a fresh assault on the people, but Echezo steps out of the crowd to face him]
Echezo:	Leave the people alone and arrest me alone. I will reveal the whole truth.
Sergeant:	You are already under arrest, you fool! You are the one who used to be in the palace, yes? Who really are you?
Echezo:	The man who can tell you everything that happened from start to finish!
	[A buzz of excitement and curiosity sweeps through the crowd. Sergeant rushes at him with a raised baton]
Sergeant:	You knew and kept quiet?

Echezo:	If you beat any of us again, I shall speak no more. Beatings cannot force a single word out of my mouth. My confession is by choice.
Sergeant:	We were asking the question . . . . Asking and asking! Why didn't you speak up? What took you so long?
Echezo:	I drank a terrible oath of secrecy to protect the dark secret in my mouth. But my heart is bleeding for these innocent people and I choose to spit everything out and rather die.
Sergeant:	So, where is the body of the white man?
Echezo:	Which one are you looking for? The white man or his body?
Sergeant:	What do you mean by that stupid question? Where is the body of the white man?
Echezo:	You will see the body when you see the white man.

> [*Excited buzz in the crowd; Sergeant is very angry*]

Sergeant:	You want to mess with me?
People:	M-e-e-e-e-e-e-ss!
Echezo:	I speak a riddle here in the open. Take me to the palace and I shall make it plain.
Sergeant:	Whatever you have to report, say it before me here and now!
Echezo:	What about my oath? I will only break it once. Take me to the palace where every spoken word has a correct price.
Sergeant:	How can I just take you straight to the king when you have not told us what you have to say? It is my duty to sift every confession before the king can give it audience.

Echezo:	Not this one. It is too deep for a stranger like you. Your king will hear how the body you are looking for was taken to a shrine in the forest . . . . and how it was cut up into equal parts for the six clans of the kingdom . . . . how the hair was counted and divided . . . how the brain was crushed with spices and mixed into palm wine for a drink in the dead of night. I will name names that will make you shudder in your pants.
Sergeant:	Say no more, say no more. I'm taking you to the king straight away. Constables!

[Constables tie up Echezo's wrists]

Constable 3:	Oga Sergeant, this is our biggest breakthrough!
Sergeant:	We've just broken the highest cult in this kingdom. A secret cult of man eaters!
Constable 1:	It is what you hear in stories but think it can never be true!
Sergeant:	Now we've heard direct from the vulture's mouth! Constables! Guard this man closely. Let's bring him alive before the king.

[Exeunt all; the crowd disperses slowly, leaving two men]

1ˢᵗ man:	Man, did you hear what I heard?
2ⁿᵈ man:	Brother, I don't know what to think or believe.
1ˢᵗ man:	Is this what they do in the dark . . . . . . human flesh? I'm choking with disgust.
2ⁿᵈ man:	But something tells me that Echezo is up to something . . .
1ˢᵗ man:	What is that again? The man confessed openly. We heard his mouth direct!
2ⁿᵈ man:	Brother, words could mean a different thing when fired as weapons of war. Umudimkpa is at war with invaders.

1ˢᵗ man:	Are you trying to defend a man who confessed in public just now? Didn't you hear what I heard?
2ⁿᵈ man:	Friend, words cast diverse spells that may divide their hearers. If you believe everything you hear these days, you run mad!
1ˢᵗ man:	If you hear everything I believe now, you will choose death. Nothing is good anymore in anything. Our country has been eaten by dogs and war is coming at us on every side!
2nd man:	I can't pretend to understand it, but I am certain that a thing greater than mountains is about to happen on the mountain!

[Blackout]

ACT 4, SCENE 2

Throne Room at Umudimkpa palace. Lance Corporal, big cudgel in hand and panting from exhaustion, stands over Echezo who is stripped to the waist and seated on the floor, legs stretched out in front, wrists and ankles tied with ropes. His bare back is covered with angry weals and bruises from severe scourging but his demeanour is still defiant. Abednego swaggers around, puffing delicately on his pipe, a bottle of gin in his left armpit. From time to time he sips at his gin, smacks his lips and rinses his mouth rather noisily before downing a mouthful. Ojongo and Sergeant stand by.

Abednego:	Echezona, son of Omemgboji, do you know the power of the white man that is now in my hands? I am king and paramount ruler . . . . greater than anybody that you and your forefathers ever served in this palace. One word from me, you are dead without question, present or future!
Echezo:	My life is not yours to mock. Why do you choose to confuse yourself about who you are and what you are?
Abednego:	I could make you cry . . . . I could make you die in slow degrees of crafted pain till you beg me for your life . . . This thing that you are dying to cover with your life will dance naked in public.
Echezo:	What worse can you do to me, Anikowaa? (Let me even call you by your birth name that everyone seems to have forgotten, the name your distressed father gave you in the terrible accident of your birth when he asked the earth goddess to explain what you are.) Anikowaa, you . . .

Sergeant:	Shut up! Say king! Say king or I flog you by myself!
Abednego:	Overlook his rudeness for now, Sergeant. The whole country will holler my correct name complete with titles in the coming days. Stampede is the dance of insects when the scorpion takes the stage.
Echezo:	Reserve your threats, Anikowaa. The marching feet of the people will crush your little scorpion when the time comes.
Abednego:	Don't be a fool! I could beat okro seeds out of your mouth without even lifting a finger!
Echezo:	You still gain nothing. Your beasts have broken their savage sticks on my backsides; but what's their gain? They are the ones with fainting hearts and aching hands! You will not hear one useful word from me till you assemble the titled elders as I have demanded.

[Abednego signals and Lance Corporal exits dejectedly]

Sergeant *[openly frustrated]*:	It is like I told you, Great One; madness is native to this land. Every small rat wants to be a dead hero.
Ojongo:	I warned you beforehand that a blind rampage settles nothing. But you are the fly that knows better than the entire sky.
Sergeant:	I am the one doing the investigation! You say "don't flog them" and I say "fine, but how else can we pull out words from this kind of people?" What is my fault that I am trying to do my duty? These natives are more stubborn than goats of the hill country!
Ojongo:	This thing you call investigation, is it what captured this fellow for us? Is it your posturing

here like a wall gecko that rattled his mind and ripened words of confession in his mouth?

Sergeant *[swaggering]:* I leave it to my king to give me my due credit. Every eye has seen what I've achieved in this place . . . Is it easy? I broke the powerful cult of man eaters and we shall hear a public confession that will shake the whole world!

Ojongo *[to Abednego]:* He makes me laugh with this kind of child talk. I am almost tempted to open his eyes. Does he know what it takes to shake the hearts of the terrible and to loosen the tied tongues of horror oaths? Ojongo knows what he put in the air to make the mountains shake!

Sergeant: Put more things in the air and make these people show more respect for their king. Why should every rat and cockroach come here and talk any how before the king?

Ojongo: This man wants to confess but he wants the chiefs and titled elders to be present! What is hard about that?

Sergeant: Who is he to insist? What right has a common captive before the king?

Echezo: The right to mock adversity with silence . . . . a basic choice that no bully can stand or understand! I am a true born of Umudimkpa!

Ojongo: This is a path to nowhere, beatings which only turn everyday fools into folk heroes.

Abednego: Take the man away, Sergeant and clean him up . . . .

[Abednego sits on the chair on the dais as Sergeant prods Echezo to get up]

Abednego: I only wanted to see how much pain the goat could endure as an adult. But, Ojongo is right, I think. This age is full of idiots who have nothing to live for; all they seek every moment is an excuse to die brave . . . . Take him outside and give him a little clean-up, then bring him back.

[Exit Sergeant, sullen-faced with a still defiant Echezo]

Ojongo:
: Great One, prepare your ears. Ojongo has invoked the mighty spirits. You will hear what you will hear, names and big titles!

Abednego:
: Speak direct, Ojongo. Is it not Akaeze and Orimili?

Ojongo:
: The confession will not shout from my mouth.

Abednego:
: Give me a little tip of privilege.

Ojongo:
: A hunter must not run ahead of the hunting dog.

Abednego:
: I can't wait to tell Dio! Human flesh in soup pots, Ojongo!

Ojongo:
: Tell him whom to thank as well. Ojongo has made something greater than a night bird to fly in the night!

Abednego *[pensively]:*
: There will be no hiding place for Akaeze and Orimili Obiora if Echezo will agree to bear true witness!

Ojingo:
: Echezo will do your wish. I have set the mighty spirits on him.

Abednego:
: I am much excited. Ask Sergeant to bring him back!

[Ojongo speaks quickly to someone at the door and returns, shaking his rattles at unseen things.]

Ojongo:
: Choi! The dreaded monster must vomit in broad daylight what secret he swallowed in the dead of night!

[Re-enter Sergeant, leading Echezo back to his previous spot. Abednego nicely waves Echezo to a bench and drags a chair over to sit before him]

Abednego: Echezona, son of Omemgboji, choose wisdom . . . I can make you the richest man in this land; I can make you a high chief in my cabinet, I swear on my honour; you will take the place of any high chief you expose by name, as you confess. Which one is it, Akaeze or Orimili? Or both?

Echezo: Are you serious? You will give me their stool? Just like that?

Abednego: Just trust me, Echezo! You become Orimili . . . . or even Akaeze! Your own choice, Echezo. Which one?

Echezo *[chuckles impishly]*: The name is already hot on my tongue!

Abednego: Choose well . . . . choose well. Do you need a drink? Here, have a sip of the white man's gin. It gives you the boldness of a real madman! Have a sip.

Echezo: Not a sip! You either give me a full bottle . . . . or you give me nothing. The tale in my mouth is pure virgin.

[Enter Constables 2 and 3]

Abednego: You will get your price. Even double! Ojongo, be my witness. Two virgin bottles of the white man's gin for Echezona! Sergeant, you too have heard. He has now promised to expose the human vultures parading as high chiefs in my kingdom.

[Ojongo shakes his rattles and speaks to the four walls]

Ojongo: Let them all be named . . . . horrors who made darkness their place of abode and swallowed flesh that even vultures would not touch . . . . creatures who forgot that the eyes in the head of Ojongo are seeing beyond the abode of mortals. I seize them by the neck and put them beneath the shadow of the Great One. Ojongo has done his own part and finished it.

Echezo:

Two virgin bottles to rinse my mouth! I will sing!

Abednego:

Sergeant, get the gin very quickly! I must keep my promise.

Sergeant:

King, the four we seized from Odikpo, the smuggler, you've finished all. The last bottle is in your hand.

Abednego:

Are you telling me there's no more gin in the whole country?

Sergeant:

The local brew may be still be found, O king.

Abednego:

Only the white man's gin for the king! Raid the country once again and fetch it for me. A king must keep his promise. Two virgin bottles for Echezo.

Sergeant:

Shon! Your Highness! Consider it done!

[Re-enter Lance Corporal breathlessly]

Lance Corporal:

Oga Sergeant, trouble! Please tell king! Chief woman fell down and her body is not moving!

Abednego:

Oyidi'a?

Lance Corporal:

Yes king. She just fell . . . . like this!

Echezo *[wails]:*

High Mother! High Mo-o-ther!

Sergeant:

Is she dead?

Lance Corporal:

She is outside. Come! Come and see . . .

[General panic, Sergeant and Lance Corporal rushing out the door, followed by Constable 2.

Echezo drags himself up and hobbles along, but Constable 3 stops him]

Echezo: Anikowaa, get this dog out of my way! I must see High Mother!

Abednego *[snapping his fingers at Constable 3]:* Allow him to go, but go with him. Keep him in close watch!

Echezo *[sneering at Abednego]:* That woman must not die!

[Exit Echezo, closely guarded by Constable 3]

Abednego: Good riddance to rags. One down, two to go!

Ojongo: You need her alive. She must yield her body and live with the shame even if for one day.

Abednego: Ojongo, my skin still crawls at the mere thought of that job! I've poured blazes down my throat but there is still no fire in my body. The thing is too mean!

Ojongo: No step is mean in the upward climb of real ambition. It takes a heart of stone to stand in the place of a king. You make it seem like you fear a mere woman.

Abednego: That woman is not just a woman. Think of her age. She is a symbol.

Ojongo: A woman is a woman, and you are the only symbol that should stand in this land. Find a way to be alone with her. Where is the horn I gave you?

[Abednego fetches the horn from behind the throne. Ojongo whispers into the horn and returns it to him]

Ojongo: Hold it in your left hand and close to your heart when you face her. I must keep out of view.

[Exit Ojongo, Abednego lost in thought]

[Fade]

Act 4, Scene 3

Throne Room at the Umudimkpa Palace. Oyidi'a looking very frail and leaning on the supporting arms of Ugochi and Orimili Obiora, enters gingerly, walking with obvious pain. Echezo hobbles after them but Constables 2 and 3 close in on him and gently pull him away. Enter Abednego looking much concerned.

Abednego:	Take her straight to my bedchamber. She deserves a good rest.
Oyidi'a:	I will sit here.
Abednego:	No, mother. You need to lie down. This is an emergency . . .
Oyidi'a:	I said I will sit here.
Abednego:	But my place is all yours, mother. The bed in that room is a dream in the clouds. From the white man's country!
Oyidi'a *[to Ugochi]:*	Help me to that common bench, my dear.
Ugochi:	High Mother, I don't think you can sit up yet.
Oyidi'a:	I will lean my back against the wall . . . . It's just a passing fever . . . . My strength will return.
Ugochi:	I will sit beside you till you are strong again.
Oyidi'a:	Thank you, my daughter.
	[With assistance, Oyidi'a sits, leaning her back on the wall, Ugochi by her side, providing a wedge]

Abednego *[to Orimili Obiora]:*   Why can't you be a man and control your
wife?

Orimili Obiora: You are not referring to me, I hope?

Abednego: Your name is still Obiora and I will not forget it
if anything goes wrong here!

Orimili Obiora: I don't know what you mean by that.

Abednego: If anything happens to High Mother, you will
know by force!

Orimili Obiora *[to no one]:*   What is he talking about?

Abednego: Umuachala cannot come into this palace and
be dictating to Umudimkpa how to take care of
our own mother. I gave up my bed so she can
have the best of rest, but you are standing here
and watching your wife spoil everything. There
will be trouble if anything happens to High
Mother.

Oyidi'a: This is about me, not you, Anikowaa; so, I will
say something for myself . . . and you must listen
very well.

Abednego: I am listening, High Mother.

Oyidi'a: I don't know what next is breeding in the inside
of your evil heart. But heaven and earth will bear
me witness this day. It is your own head . . . your
own very head . . . that will carry the ground
from deep under before I turn my back.

Ugochi: Ise-ee!

Abednego: Ah, High Mother, your words are unkind to my
thoughts of you . . . .

Oyidi'a: You have not even heard an inch of the mile.

Abednego: But I still have a pleasant surprise for you. As it
looks though, it has to wait for a better moment
of privacy.

Oyidi'a:	Privacy? You and me? Never, Anikowaa! Not on your life! I'll never sit in any private meeting with something of your type.
Abednego:	I can never fault your judgment, High Mother. But what I have for your ears cannot wait for too long and time is running out. It won't be fair for anyone to blame me later.
Oyidi'a:	Then, out with it. Speak now and let me hear.
Abednego:	High Mother, this matter concerns Igwe the Sky-king himself, our great father. I can't treat it as everyday tittle-tattle that brush the ears of busybodies. I'd rather wait till you are stronger . . . and we can have a quiet moment together . . . . at your own time and place.
Oyidi'a:	If it is anything about my dear husband, I want to hear it now.
Abednego:	High Mother, the matter is for your ears only. It is deep.

[Oyidi'a gently taps Orimili and Ugochi]

Oyidi'a:	Spare me a moment with him.
Orimili Obiora:	Ah, High Mother!
Ugochi:	What do you want to hear from a rattlesnake?
Oyidi'a:	Don't worry about me, child.
Ugochi:	High Mother, I am not going to leave you alone with this creature even for one eye-blink.
Oyidi'a:	You will do so, because I ask you to . . .
Orimili Obiora:	We shall obey your wish, Oyidi'a . . . . but . . . . you can feel our utmost reluctance. We shall keep within earshot.
Abednego:	Earshot! What you want to hear, is it meant for your ears? Why don't you ever know where you are not wanted?

Orimili Obiora:	Oyidi'a, we shall be watching out for your safety.
Oyidi'a:	Don't make me feel like a crawling baby that must be looked after by everybody.
Ugochi:	This fellow is poison, High Mother . . . . and you are unwell!
Oyidi'a:	I can take care of myself. I killed a serpent or two long before this one was born. Let me hear what he has to say of my late husband.

[Exeunt Orimili and Ugochi reluctantly]

Abednego:	Well . . . . I've been called all sorts of bad names, right from my infancy. None of that bothers me really, High Mother, because the noisemakers cannot tell a sheep from a goat much less a man from an ape. But when you, High Mother, the only woman I adore in this whole world, join them in calling me a snake, the tears sting my eyes . . . . But I am not going to cry here. I must speak to correct some wrong impressions.
Oyidi'a:	What wrong impressions, Anikowaa? Please don't waste your breath and my precious time. Go straight to my husband's matter or I walk out of here.
Abednego:	You will hear me, High Mother, because you are the mother I never had. It was you I ran to every time in those terrible days. You may no longer remember but I will never forget your steadying hand in my life; when sorrows gripped my infant heart and floods of tears set themselves to cut me off, you alone were there for me. I grew up swimming against the tides of passion in a world that hated this one little child. It was only you and your great husband, Igwe, the Sky-king, who gave me the lamp of love that even a father refused to show me. I did not know then the big

truth that I now know, so it was very difficult for this small boy.

Oyidi'a: The small boy then came of age and turned himself into an odious monster. What is your life, Anikowaa? It is nothing but a grudge fight against all creation. Go ahead with it; crush your mates . . . . wipe out your seniors . . . Please go to the subject of our discussion.

Abednego: Hear me, High Mother. Why is it that devilish lies are easier to believe than divine truths? All manner of lies . . . lies in their desperate thousands . . . were told against my person in these past twenty years. Everything gone wrong with my generation has been blamed on my head . . . . because I was not around, and nobody spoke for me.

Oyidi'a: What drove you away like an evil dog that must keep running and running? Is it not your own atrocities? Who will ever forget your evil mind? You tried to poison an entire council of high chiefs that included your own father!

Abednego *[feigning shock]*: So you too believe that story? Oh, High Mother . . . you too? *[sinks to his knees, covers his face and sobs]* Then my case is hopeless . . . . So many lies, so many lies against me . . . . everybody against one orphan child . . . . because he has no father, no mother!

[Oyidi'a is moved . . . she looks confused]

Oyidi'a: Anikowaa, you cannot say that.

Abednego: I am saying it, I'm saying it! How could you, High Mother? How could you believe that I would poison anybody? You are the mother I never had . . . . I thought you were there for me!

Oyidi'a:	Are you telling me that what happened did not happen? That what all Umudimkpa is saying is not true?

[Abednego rises, sits dejectedly on a bench]

Abednego:	It's been twenty years of torture. Every day, I've mourned that boy, Ifediba and wished that he had even the little courage to stay alive. Only he could have told the world the very advice I gave him, the truth that he ignored and put us all in this mess . . . . I don't want to sound like I'm lying against the dead.
Oyidi'a:	My brain is tired. I don't know what to remember or forget in what you are saying.
Abednego:	High Mother, I always thought you were there for me. The thought of you was like a shining lamp in the pitch darkness of twenty years in which I roamed the wild world like a castaway. There were moments of anguish so intense I thought of taking my own life to end the misery. But I would hear your gentle voice asking me to come home . . . . You urged me to ignore the riot of accusations . . . . You said to me 'be a man, return home . . . prove your innocence.' You talked to me tenderly like nobody ever did. So much love, so much sweetness and fairness . . . . and faith in me . . . It was your words that kept me alive and guided me home. Without you, I would be lost for ever . . .
Oyidi'a:	My head is pounding . . . . I'm getting . . . . dizzy again. See, we can continue later . . . Call Ugochi for now . . . . Call her quickly.

[Abednego rushes to her side]

Abednego:	Please don't die, High Mother . . . . Give me a chance to show how much I care for you . . . . I am the son you never had. I love you so very much!

[He caresses her neck and shoulders, inching down slowly to her breasts. Oyidi'a's eyes are closed]

Oyidi'a *[gives a sudden start]:*   What is this? What are you doing?

Abednego: Take me as your son . . . . I came home for your sake . . . . I must take special care of you . . . . Special, special care of you . . . . But, what I still don't understand, High Mother—Why did you join them in covering the truth from me?

Oyidi'a: What truth was covered?

Abednego: The truth about my real father. Why didn't anyone tell me who my real father was?

Oyidi'a: Your real father? What is the meaning of that one? Ah, my head is breaking . . .

Abednego: Every child deserves to know his father.

Oyidi'a: But you knew your father . . . . Everyone knew your father . . . .

Abednego: Everyone believed that Dikeogu was my father . . . .

Oyidi'a: My head! My head! I don't know what you are saying . . .

Abednego: You must lie down in bed, High Mother. Please permit me to carry you to bed.

Oyidi'a: Nobody carries me to bed . . . . Ask Ugochi to come back . . . here . . . quickly.

[Abednego heads to the door, stops and returns]

Abednego: The man who called himself my father hated me so much! You know why, don't you?

Oyidi'a: Why are you bringing up a dead matter? Call Ugochi for me . . . . I am feeling very dizzy now . . . .

Abednego:	Ugochi . . . . she is on her way . . . . I was speaking of that man, Dikeogu. Why did all you elders support him against me?
Oyidi'a:	Dikeogu is your father! Nobody can blame him . . . . in your matter. You gave him too much trouble . . . .
Abednego:	He disowned me.
Oyidi'a:	Your misdeeds forced his hand.
Abednego:	He was not my father. He hated me . . . . A father cannot hate his son . . . That man hated me; but Igwe loved me! I used to wonder why. I never knew the answer until Igwe himself came to me in a dream and explained things to me. Three good times, I dreamt that dream in the last few months. He told me everything . . . Then my eyes cleared! Are you there, High Mother? Can you still hear me?

[Oyidi'a is sagging. Abednego touches her and she slumps to the floor. He anxiously feels her pulse and heartbeat, then beams with smiles, flexing his muscles. Enter Ojongo]

Ojongo:	Be quick; into your chamber. She's all yours!
Abednego:	I'm still not sure I can do this. My body feels nothing.
Ojongo:	Drink hard; fire up yourself ; be a man!
Abednego:	I've almost emptied my last bottle. Still, I feel nothing.
Ojongo:	The fire will come when you take off her clothes. Be a man.

[Abednego drains the bottle and drops it]

Abednego:	Give me a hand.
Ojongo:	She is all yours. Waste no time

[They carry Oyidi'a inside the bedroom and Ojongo comes hurrying back.]

Ojongo *[Aside, impishly]:* '*Tufiaa*' was her own language!

[Fade]

Act 4, Scene 4

Throne Room at Umudimkpa Palace. Sergeant knocks on the door of Abednego's bedchamber. Ojongo is seated in the near corner, thumbing tobacco snuff into his nostrils. A crowd is heard in the distance singing "Akweke Olima"

Sergeant:*[shifting about uncomfortably]*: This is an emergency! He has to wake up. You say he is lying naked on the floor . . . . I have no permit to see him like that . . . .

Ojongo: So, knock harder. Knock like you have the fist of a grown-up!

Sergeant *[pounds on the door]*: You are wrong, Ojongo! A blame that falls on my head will never perch a feathered cap on yours. Help wake him up now because there is big trouble!

Ojongo: I told you what I told you. A head full of strong liqueur has no ear for wake-up calls!

Sergeant *[pounds harder on the door]*: Why is nobody telling me what happened here? What was that tumult about?

Ojongo: When the king is up, he will answer for himself.

Sergeant *[exasperatedly]*: But your natives are massing up on the square like a crowd of lunatics. You can hear them chanting abuses. If they storm the palace, we are badly outnumbered. We need the king's orders to shoot!

Ojongo:	You never told anybody that it is an invasion with bows and arrows, machetes, spears and other dangerous weapons.
Sergeant:	I never said they have weapons . . .
Ojongo:	So what is the cry about?
Sergeant:	I know what I fear. Certain things look like nothing whilst they carry lethal power. Every one out there is holding a broom.
Ojongo:	I'll be first to agree that a broom can be more dangerous than any weapon; but never mind, Sajent man, there are still ordinary brooms for sweeping.
Sergeant:	How can we tell the difference? Trouble makers carry brooms everywhere these days and they want to sweep every place. Hear their chants. They see defilement everywhere!

[Enter Abednego, somewhat groggy, with a loud sneeze]

Abednego:	Defilement is the very word! . . . . *[a big wide yawn]* . . . Dogs of defilement! That's what they are. Dogs we took as men! Ah, my head is being hammered . . . I shouldn't be talking much. *[sits down heavily]* . . . . Who can imagine that high chiefs in this land sat down and ate a man? Those are dogs and must be rounded up and hanged! Have you re-arrested them, Sergeant?
Sergeant:	King, we have an emergency!
Abednego:	There is nothing called emergency when there is no more fight! Think in the head, Sergeant. Their fight-back is over.
Sergeant:	King, there is a big crowd out there refusing to disperse. That is an emergency. We need your orders to shoot.

Abednego:	Bring me Akaeze and Orimili Obiora. No need to shoot a gun!
Sergeant:	King, the whole place is blocked. It's miles of angry people!
Abednego:	Arrest Akaeze and Orimili. What is a legion once the head is cut off? It is nothing! Where is that Echezona? Bring him to expose the man-eaters before the people!

[Enter Lance Corporal]

Lance Corporal:	Shon sir! King sir, the crowd is marching on the palace!
Sergeant:	Relax, Corp'l. King says relax.
Lance Corporal:	But they have brooms in their hands!
Abednego:	Brooms? *[in sudden panic]* Ojongo, brooms again? Brooms!
Ojongo:	Those are normal brooms, Great One . . . .
Abednego:	Normal what? Move, Sergeant! If you have to shoot, shoot everybody!
Ojongo:	Great One, that crowd is just women and children.
Abednego:	Anyone with a broom is an enemy. Shoot, Sergeant!

[Enter Echezo, hands still tied]

Echezo:	No need to shoot. If I can play the palace *ekwe,* the people will disperse.
Abednego:	Echezona, you will drink appreciation from my royal horn for the rest of your life. That *ekwe* is your first act in your new office when you finish playing and name your title.
Echezo:	My eyes will lead my dance of the heart. Tell them to untie my hands. They can tie me back when I drop the sticks.

[He holds out his ropes and at a nod from Abednego, Lance Corporal unties his wrists and ankles]

Abednego: Quick with it! Stop their howling. I hate that mad song!

[Exit Echezo, Lance Corporal following]

Ojongo: Unless you round up the ringleaders, distractions will continue.

Abednego: Sergeant is too slow! That is my headache in everything. What is so hard in arresting two useless chiefs?

Sergeant: Shon king! my men have gone to bring them . . .

Abednego: I want to see the look on their faces when their recipe of the deepest night is thrown open to the whole world.

Sergeant: Shon sir! I will go personally now and get them myself.

[Exit Sergeant]

Abednego: Sergeant is too slow! I have a bad headache . . . .

[The ekwe limbers up, slow at first, then quickens in tone and tempo. The crowd chanting of 'Akweke Olima' subsides]

Abednego: Only the *ekwe* could kill off that noise so quickly . . . . How long had they been singing that nonsense?

Ojongo: Quite a while, Great One. You slept like you were dead. I had to boil some very rare herbs to call you back to life.

Abednego: But brooms again, Ojongo? Are we not done with brooms?

Ojongo: Great One, that gathering is harmless.

Abednego:	Harmless, Ojongo? Brooms?
Ojongo:	It is just the customary labour which the womenfolk perform on the palace grounds from time to time with their younger children. Somebody just shows them where to sweep and when to stop.
Abednego:	I don't want brooms in this palace. No brooms anymore! No brooms! And that's final!
Ojongo:	The *ekwe* has already told them to leave; they would disperse. Brooms can be symbolic anyway.
Abednego:	What is called symbolic? The people are very stupid . . . . or they have no useful work to do. Imagine carrying brooms about! From now on, anybody who steps into the palace grounds with that thing in hand will get shot like a bush fowl!
Ojongo:	Great One, let's talk of . . . . yourself and Oyidi'a.
Abednego:	What do you want to hear again?
Ojongo:	You know what about . . . . Did you do it?
Abednego *[pensive awhile]*:	I can't seem to remember . . . . True . . . . My head is fuzzy and heavy. I have a bad headache.
Ojongo:	I had to cook things to wake you up. You were out cold . . . naked on the bare floor.
Abednego:	Who else saw me like that?
Ojongo:	Orimili was there before me. It was he and Echezo that carried Oyidi'a away.
Abednego:	Obiora saw me naked?
Ojongo:	His wife too would have seen an eyeful if I did not quickly cover your body before she came in.

Abednego:	Where were my bodyguards? And where was Sergeant?
Ojongo:	You still believe in those jokers in uniform to guard your life?
Abednego:	But where were they? Where did they go?
Ojongo:	You sent them on a raid for more hot drinks, if I remember. I hear they found some at the grieving house of Oche-ilo-eze.
Abednego:	I need another drink . . . . I must clear my head.

[Sits down heavily on a bench]

Ojongo:	My question is how did that girl find a way into your bedroom?
Abednego:	Which girl?
Ojongo:	The one who screamed for the whole world to hear! The lass, Akweke.
Abednego:	Akweke . . . in my room? Yes, I now remember . . . . She was the one! Yes! She was the one!
Ojongo:	The one who did what? What did you do with that girl after my repeated warnings to you? Chei! Great One! I warned you . . . .
Abednego:	I did not touch her . . . . And I still don't know how she emerges at will from her cell of detention because if you go even now, you'll find her tightly tied to a huge pole there.
Ojongo:	So, what was her mission in your bedroom?
Abednego:	I thought I was alone with only a half-conscious old woman. My own bedroom . . . . The door was well secured . . . . and my servants had my clear orders to keep everyone off, including themselves . . . . I think I had removed my clothes . . . The next thing I remember, that girl

was standing before me and screaming to the high heavens. She is a bad witch, Ojongo . . . . I'm going to kill her . . . . and nobody should stop me!

Ojongo: But where was the horn I gave you to hold?

Abednego: How can I remember a horn? Everything was one big pool of darkness and I was falling headlong into a bottomless pit!

Ojongo: It must be the power of liqueur. You had too much of it.

Abednego: No, Ojongo, it is witchcraft. I know a witch when I see one. That girl must show me what I want to see. Where is she now?

Ojongo: She melted away in the general confusion.

Abednego: She will not go like that because I'm not done with her. I must discover the alleyway to her strange power. No woman in this world will put me down and buzz off to sing like a bird.

Ojongo: For one who has a full stable of the finest mares, what is one small rabbit that you cannot allow her to pass by?

Abednego: What I need from you is power to ride. Leave me to advise myself which horse or donkey, rat or rabbit!

Ojongo: Great One, a great kingdom is sprawled out before you, like a waiting bride. But royalty is its own best advisor.

Abednego: Indeed I have advised myself and I've chosen what I've chosen. The throne for power and that girl for final proof.

Ojongo: Final proof of what, Great One?

Abednego: I speak no further on that subject.

[Enter Lance Corporal dragging Akweke in ropes]

Lance Corporal: King sir! The witch girl was trying to escape again! But I say no way, she cannot!

Abednego: Lock her up! Lock her up!

Akweke: Monkey will yet curse the fate that pushed him to wrestle Baboon. Agbala! Your daughter is in ropes! Abomination!

Abednego: Lock her up! Tie her with strongest ropes and lock her up!

Akweke: Agbala! Let your revenge strike without missing. The bastard who dared your hill must not live to boast of it! Prove yourself for your daughter's sake! Agbala!

[Exit Lance Corporal dragging Akweke by the ropes on her wrists. Re-enter Sergeant, saluting]

Sergeant: More troops from Ubulu, O king. Twelve men with rifles!

Abednego: That is good news. That is very good news.

Sergeant: A letter by the hand of the troop leader.

[Abednego receives the letter, a brown envelope]

Abednego: From D.O. himself. Ha, ha! Dio, Dio! *[hands trembling; he manages some flourish as he opens the envelope. He sits on the edge of his chair and proceeds to read aloud in the stilted, halting manner of a half-literate rustic]*

Abednego *[reading]:* From: The District Office, Ubulu Native Administration Authority,

To: The Warrant Chief designate and *Tigbulu Efi Togbolu Mgbede*, Abednego I of Umudimkpa

Abednego *[aside]:*   Which one is Warrant Chief again? Paramount
                        Ruler is what I like to be called. It is a better
                        sound and it fills the mouth that calls it as it fills
                        the ear that hears it!

                        *[Mr Barnsley's voice-over conveys the rest of the
                        letter]*

Mr Barnsley's *voice:*

I have pleasure in writing to inform you that I have
dispatched to your domain a fresh squad of twelve men
with loaded rifles. Their immediate deployment should
secure the peace and curb the last fringes of tension which
could pose a grave threat to law and order.

The District Office has noted your excellent performance
in tax remittance in these few days and in spite of the
grave security situation of the moment in your territory.
I urge you to sustain the drive with a view to improving
even further on the returns. I should be in a position very
shortly, to communicate a date for your coronation and
the formal presentation of your certificate of office.

I am, however, much distressed by the grave allegations in
your dispatches regarding poor Rev. J. D. Jones. I need you
to personally recheck and verify your facts as a full-scale
punitive expedition is bound to follow if this outrageous
report is confirmed to be true. The matter is so grave
that I need must respond with an instant order not only
to round up the members of that nefarious cult but also
to punish the offending community with due severity.
However, I have just received from Hezekiah a rather
confusing note by reason of which I am constrained for
now, to put the expedition on hold until I receive your
express clarification.

Let me therefore hear from you very urgently, the exact
truth of this very grave matter.

                                        Yours faithfully
                                        Harvey J. Barnsley
                                        Ag District Officer

Abednego:	Sergeant, quick, arrest that idiot they call Hezekiah, now!
Sergeant:	What offence, O King?
Abednego:	Think in the head! Hezekiah must come and tell us who gave him power to write to Dio? I am king and when I write to Dio, then Hezekiah gets up and writes too! Who born dog?
Sergeant:	I did not know he wrote anything, O king.
Abednego:	You never know anything until I put it in your eye by myself!
Sergeant:	I will teach that rat, king! Allow me to handle him for you!
Abednego:	Because of him, Dio is saying grave, grave. This letter is full of grave! Which grave? My own letter to Dio was very clear that bad mouths have eaten his brother! But Hezekiah has written a big lie to him that there is a grave.
Sergeant:	He is trying to be too clever. I will finish him by myself.
Ojongo [to Abednego]:	Great one, the gods are not happy at all with that one you call 'Ezekaya. Be very careful with him. Very, very careful.
Abednego:	He is the one to be careful after what I will do to him. Where is he by the way? What has he been doing since his master died?
Ojongo:	I heard that he took up with Ogbuefi Iwobi. Even that one too is new trouble. He now goes about talking nonsense how the white man healed him by something he calls miracle.
	[Ojongo whispers something into Abednego's ears and he nods vigorously]

Abednego:	You have my consent, Ojongo. Absolutely! Do whatever you want to him and his family! Stupid people! Miracle!

[Exit Ojongo]

Abednego:	And you, Sergeant, think in the head. Why did Hezekiah tell such a blatant lie? Why is he claiming that there is a grave when the whole land knows that there is no grave?
Sergeant:	King, I think Hezekiah is hiding something. It is like he knows the very people who ate the white man!
Abednego:	Can't you see he is one of them? Dio wants me to check the whole matter by myself. Bring all the cult members here . . . . and be very quick with it! My problem with you is you are too slow.

[A burly stranger fills the doorway. He is barefooted, dressed in extra-large khaki shorts and shirt with front brass buttons and his head is bandaged to cover his left eye]

Stranger:	That problem is over. The man who swallows before anyone can chew is here!
Sergeant:	Who allowed you to walk into this place? Who are you?
Stranger:	I am Okpijo, the lobster who forbids peace as sickness and chooses war for handshake!
Abednego:	Okpijo! Is this you? Evil Prawn that only thrives in combat!
Okpijo:	Sell me, a bag of money; kill me, a pot of meat!
Abednego:	Okpijo! *Atakata Agboa!* The endless chaw that wearies the jaws and forces the mouth to spit him out!
Okpijo:	White man's prison is the latest to spit me out at long last. It was only yesterday; they told me

that I was now free to go and serve the new king of Umudimkpa. *[Prostrates totally on the floor]* King, see your servant on the floor. Ask me up and every whisperer against you is a dead rat in this land.

Abednego: Rise up, Okpijo. With immediate effect, you are in charge of Special Duties!

Okpijo: Special Duties! I like the sound of it.

Abednego: Sergeant, inform your men immediately. We now have Special Duties, the unit who will move things and people the way I want. There must be full cooperation and no questions! Let your men understand fully well that there must be no questions! This is Okpijo, the strongman who accepts no sorry!

Sergeant: Shon sir!

Abednego: You will continue with your police work but leave all special duties to him.

Sergeant: All correct, sir! But King sir, which of the jobs are called Special Duties?

Abednego: Didn't you hear No Questions? Think in the head!

Sergeant: Shon sir, king! No complaint! Permission to go for Hezekiah!

[Exit Sergeant]

Abednego: Your coming is timely. There is work that cannot wait.

Okpijo: It's been in my mind to talk about it because I noticed too many people here who are shooting eyes at things that are not their business. A few serious slaps will settle that aspect.

Abednego: Okpijo, this matter is bigger than slapping people. We are about to tear the masks of deceit off the faces of Akaeze and Obiora, son of Orimili. Umudimkpa will shake today.

Okpijo:

That boy Obiora and his adopted father, Akaeze . . . they were the main reason I left this kingdom. They used to look at me like I was dog shit! Anything to scar their faces, leave it to me.

Abednego:

Come, I'll explain what you must do.

[Lance Corporal bursts in, worriedly]

Lance Corporal:

King, sir, that girl again, Akweke! She has entered your bedroom again!

Abednego:

Did you not tie her in that cell? Didn't you bar the door?

Lance Corporal:

King, we even used the iron clamp this time. Nothing can hold that girl, king. She is a true witch, my King!

Abednego:

Okpijo, see my trouble?

Okpijo:

A witch?

Abednego:

Evil on two legs, Okpijo.

Okpijo:

But she's a woman?

Abednego:

One small girl but by her own confession a dangerous snake . . . . Now, she enters my bedroom.

Okpijo:

I am going in there straight. Lock the door on me and her.

[Exit Okpijo, Lance Corporal following nervously]

[Fade]

ACT 4, SCENE 5

The King's public square at Umudimkpa is filling up steadily and heavy security is visible in the number of stern-looking armed troops taking charge of proceedings. The palace ekwe resounds with deep throaty threnody and warning blasts, then settles into a muted engagement. Ebili is heading towards the stage from the back of the audience, hands in front, wrists tied together, an armed guard giving him a perfunctory shove now and then. He loudly declaims the ekwe monologue, stopping in his tracks from time to time for good effect . . .

Ebili *[declaiming, line by line]*:
Cooked and corked, cooked and all loaded
Clouded and compounded, darkening to a finish

Call mother to come, call father to enter
Call the alien child, be he dwarf or giant
To set the cooking pot in the evil forest
Dog's head of vengeance, a count of how many
What benevolence is adequate for a world of grief?

The truth of coconut is sap and tasty pulp
Let the spider mind his web, the weaverbird his nest

On stage is an assembly of eminent elders, mostly ozo *titled men with eagle feathered caps. Five* odu *women, wearing their emblems of title (ivory wristlets and anklets) are separately seated. Everyone looks subdued and listless. Sitting is on rows of wooden benches, all facing an imposing cane chair adorned with white cloth on a podium. The atmosphere is very tense and rather awkward; ubiquitous armed guards perform their duties with a no-nonsense attitude that results in one or two brushes and skirmishes. Ebili is marched to the front row to stand by the side just as three gunshots in short measured intervals raise heartbeats. A loud bell is rung; Ojongo steps in as herald, a heavy bell in his hand.*

Ojongo: Country hear! Country hear me well! Your king is here! Your very king is here! He has entered (Obatago abata!) The Tagbulu Efi, Togbolu Mgbede! The Tigbulu Enyi, Tigbulu Anyinya! The Mkpufia Aru, Obodo Ana Ebe! The Ogonogo Mkpu Ana Eti Acha Acha! King that the white man himself has given paper! Ogbu Wala Wala n'Onwee Nya! Paramount ruler of all Umudimkpa, Eze Abadinegwu Nke Mbu . . . .

[Abednego marches to the platform, his countenance grim, his manner gruff, cow horn in his right hand]

Ojongo: Thunder does not beg silence to hear the end of whispers!

Abednego: Umudimkpa must forgive the frown on my face. Your own frown will be deeper trenches when you hear what you will hear just now . . . . An abomination which can wipe out the whole country has been committed in our midst. Today, we must hand over the guilty ones to Dio for punishment. According to law that is written in the white man's book, they must die by hanging; but it is for the white man himself to hang them. If we hide them, Umuachala will repeat here because the white man's anger will eat everybody's head. We must not hide anybody no matter his rank, age or title. Anyone who brings death, let him carry it upon his own head alone!

Ojongo: Speak it strong, Great One! Speak it very strong!

Abednego: You are the worthiest people in this land and I have specially selected you to be here today as face witnesses. Many heads are better in judging a strange thing because a baby snake sighted by only one person may seem a whole python.

Today you will make up your own minds where you are going with us, whether up or down because very soon, the *Nsugbe* coconut will be broken here, before your very eyes.

Ojongo:

Speak it strong, Great One! Let them hear full and well! Bite no words!

Abednego:

For full twenty years, too many lies were told, too many truths gagged or strangled. But today, the truth will leap out of the pit of denials and celebrate itself in open confession. We must save our country! Our heritage shall be delivered today from the vain clutches of small minds who found themselves in high positions but shamed our collective trust in a manner that belittled us all. This is the end of the road for beasts of infamy, jokers we exalted in ignorance and honoured in gross error. Never again will those who eat strange meats in the dead of night wipe their lips in our face with morning smiles of deceit.

Ojongo:

Knock it in, Great One. Let even the deaf hear!

Abednego:

Umudimkpa, be my witness. I have not opened my mouth to accuse anybody. I was not there when they did what they did. But someone was there with them when they did it. He will tell us how they did what they did. Bring the witness!

Ebili *[to no one]:*

How they did what? What is called what they did? Has it no name, what they did?

[A repressed buzz goes through the assembly]

Abednego *[coldly]:*

You stand before your betters like a captive slave; and your rope of shame should be your first question of sanity.

Ebili:

Not when madness is doing all the talking and must have all the answers!

[Another buzz. Abednego shifts angrily]

Abednego:	Insolence is a boast of courage in the mouth of a fool!
Ebili:	That's a dangerous truth . . . . in the best mouth to say it.

[Abednego sits down angrily, on the cane chair]

Abednego *[to no one]:*	Where is Okpijo? *[bristling]* Where is he?

[Enter Sergeant, leading Echezo with bound wrists to stand beside Ebili]

Sergeant *[salutes]:*	Shon sir!
Abednego:	Sergeant, I want Okpijo here now. But meanwhile, the best of Umudimkpa are what you see before you. Tell them why the white man wants to come and burn down this country!
Sergeant:	It is because of the bad thing by some bad people, very wicked of them. After killing the white preacher, insult on injury!
Abednego:	Tell them, Sergeant. Tell them everything!
Sergeant:	Egbuna your native is who killed white man; that is enough to kill off everybody; but that one is a small matter now because a major trouble has come. Your people have done a thing that is dirty to hear in the ear. For the sake of juju, they gathered in secret like evil vultures and ate the body of the white man!

[Expressions of dismay and disgust, the assembly on its feet, many vocal in their protests, the guards striving to restore order]

Abednego *[smiling indulgently]:* Decent people anywhere would react exactly as you have just done . . . . because this is not just another horror story. It is a nightmare that emptied my bowels as painfully as my own refusal to believe it gave me a constipation. But hear the names first. Tell them, Sergeant.

Sergeant:	There is nothing one hand buries that another hand cannot dig up. Whether High This or High That, nobody is above the white man's law that is written in a book. Bring the accused!

[Lance Corporal herds Akaeze and Orimili in, two armed guards behind them. Akaeze's face is expressionless but Orimili is evidently struggling with emotions, his hands bound at the wrists held out in despair. There are mixed reactions from the assembly—gasps, fits and starts of astonishment, outrage, bewilderment and frustration]

Abednego:	Nobody can break the law of the white man that is written in a book and go free. But whoever brings evil, it will only eat his own head and leave our Umudimkpa for us.
Ojongo:	*I see-ee*, Great One. Speak it stronger!
Abednego:	Umudimkpa must not defend anyone who does what earth itself forbids, what the sky rejects and our sleeping fathers call abomination. Two prisoners are before you, one in fetters, the other left to the damning weight of his own age. What I promise Umudimkpa is that evil will never again ride on our heads because it wears a big title!
Ebili:	Or because he's a proven bastard, disowned by his own father!
Abednego *[angrily, to Lance Coporal]:*	Take this fool away! Hand him to Special Duties!
Lance Corporal:	King sir, no one has seen Okpijo. He is still missing!
Abednego *[raging]:*	Look for him, you pig heads! Sergeant! Find that block head! And take this nuisance away!
Ebili *[jubilant, raises his bound wrists]:*	Umudimkpa, mind your goats! This is not about a dead white man; it is your

	goats, live goats! The dead man is only an excuse!
Lance Corporal:	Order!
Ebili:	Odour! Shouting that thing, does it change the truth? First, you steal goats from their owners; then you steal ropes from the goats; then you tie the owners with ropes you stole from their goats. What is happening to our goats? That's my question! The goats, Umudimkpa! The live goats, not the dead man!

[Ebili is dragged away by Sergeant and Lance Corporal]

Abednego:	A full-time drunk sees alike with a madman but has a louder voice of confusion! We are talking a serious matter of life and death. Someone is shouting goat! Reverend Jones was a white man and a very good man. He came to us in peace but he was killed by a bad boy who has run away. If he was not killed, would we be here? If it was only a gunshot wound and he survived it, who would blame Umudimkpa, and what case has *gorment*? It is that man's death . . . . that man's painful death! That is the beginning of this trouble!
Ojongo:	But only the beginning, Great One. Only the small part!
Abednego:	Isn't that clear to every adult? The father of all trouble is this ugly matter that is filling our ears—that two of our high chiefs went in the dead of night and ate the dead body!

[The assembly goes into tumult again, everyone on their feet and talking at the same time]

| Constable: | Order! Silence everywhere! |

[The guards join the general attempt to restore order, everyone telling everyone else to calm down.

Ogbuefi Ekwegbalu—tall and middle-aged, a long staff in hand, remains standing as the noise dies down]

Ogbuefi Ekwegbalu: What we are hearing is too serious to be swallowed in total silence. We must have evidence . . . . or the guns that are now pointing at only two heads must shoot down a lot more people . . . . starting from me here!

Abednego: Even a stranger knows of the courage in Umudimkpa, that it speaks out of every grain of sand. But I am not here to push threats with anyone. What you have heard about the white man's body, do you think it was invented? Two chiefs ate the dead body! That is the plain truth . . . . and there was an eye witness, and he is here with us! Echezo, speak for yourself, and hold nothing back.

[Echezo steps forward, hands bound in ropes]

Echezo: My fathers and mothers, titled and knitted, owners of my country, my knees are on the ground and my words are unrehearsed. *[He kneels awhile, then rises]* I saw my country deep in distress, death and blood at every doorstep, sudden graves eating up the farmlands. Nobody spoke to neighbour or kinsman and there was neither meeting nor meeting place.

Abednego: Echezo, what are you saying? Go straight to the point.

Echezo: Where else am I going? The words chase themselves because my head is empty. I've lost count of the dead and dying, overnight burials and no mourning even for chiefs and titled elders, every dead dumped like nameless refuse into hurried pits. The dust of defeat is so strange in these parts that now everyone seems to be blinded to the whirlwind of reprisals that is pushing insanity to kill us all . . . .

Abednego: Echezo, what happened to the body of the white man? Get to that point!

Echezo: Anikowaa, if you won't let me talk, I will stop. But if you want me to say what I have to say, you must let me get there my own way. I am Echezona, son of Omemgboji and I earned the right to speak to this assembly because I took beatings for it.

Abednego: Talk . . . . nobody is stopping you; but just make it short! You can't take for ever!

Echezo: Somebody must tell our people to stop defeating themselves. The strength of Umudimkpa is when it agrees on a matter. It may take long meetings and strong debates but we always eat agreement as fruit and take it home with us . . . and we live by it. But where has Umudimkpa held any meeting lately? Is the kingdom not facing its worst crisis of all time? Echezona, son of Omemgboji has a duty in the palace. He's the one who plays the king's *ekwe* to summon important meetings, but as you can see, his hands are tied at this time. So, now you know why he has played a different kind of instrument. It is the same result: The meeting is summoned and here it is.

[General excitement, puzzled glances etc, everyone speaking at the same time. Ojongo confers with Abednego]

Abednego *[furious and menacingly deliberate]:* Echezona! Who ate the body of the white man?

Echezo: I told you I must make a public confession. That is a promise I repeat before everyone here. But if this is a real meeting of our people, should a free-born of Umudimkpa suffer ropes in the sight of his kinsmen? Let's tell ourselves the native truth!

[He holds out his bound wrists. Abednego looks frustrated, hisses uncomfortably]

Abednego *[snapping his fingers at Constable 2]:*   Untie him.

Echezo *[turning away and indicating Orimili]:*   Him   first,   stranger. That's a high chief of the land!

Abednego *[jumping to his feet]:*   No, he stays tied! And you are the one that must explain why! *[Shaking uncontrollably]* Tell Umudimkpa what you know. Say it short and simple. No more long speeches! Who ate the white man's body?

Echezo: Straight answer is two high chiefs!

[The assembly goes abuzz with consternation. Abednego poses big with a matter-of-fact shrug and a telling grin]

Ojongo *[shaking his rattles at the four cardinal points]:*   Choi! The smell has reported the content of the pot! What is the heavy lid still battling to hide? Mist of dawn, dust of sunset, remember what you have eaten from my hand . . . . Hide nothing! Choi!

Abednego: Umudimkpa, your own ears have heard and now you know why the white man's army is about to march upon our heads. But this kingdom is not foolish. We will not die for the sake of two shameless men who are vultures in disguise!

Ogbuefi Ekwegbalu *[rising to his feet]:*   Echezona, I call you by your name, son of Omemgboji! Are you standing before Umudimkpa to say what I have just heard, that Akaeze and Orimili who we see here alive and breathing before us, ate a dead body? That is, they took a dead man's flesh with their hands, put it in their mouths, chewed it as meat, and swallowed it? And Earth allows them to stand here alive!

Echezo:	I never said it is Akaeze and Orimili.
Abednego:	Look, don't attempt to twist the confession you've already made in public! You said two high chiefs.
Ojongo:	Which else but these two? Eto'odike is confined to his sick bed; Mmanko is taken away; these are the only two high chiefs who are up and doing. Is that in dispute?
Echezo:	Now we sound like total strangers in our own land!
Ojongo:	What do you mean by that?
Echezo:	Tradition, Ojongo, tradition that we all know and observe. Is anyone taken as dead simply because his body is put in the ground and covered with sand? What happens to his spirit? Does it not stay alive, full of grief and anger, troubling the living until his relations do their duty by him?
Ogbuefi Ekwegbalu:	Yes, a funeral is a must to send home the spirit of the departed.
Echezo:	Ogbuefi Ekwegbalu, why has there been no funeral for two strongmen that Umudimkpa lost in one day, two high chiefs?
Ogbuefi Ekwegbalu:	Ajofia and Dikeogu . . . .
Echezo:	Their angry spirits are full of grief. I fear they will eat more bodies dead and alive than the body of the white man.
Abednego *[shaking with rage]:*	Ojongo, have you heard? Have you heard the nonsense in the mouth of that fool? Where is Okpijo? Somebody call that blockhead here! Where is he? Where is Okpijo?

[Re-enter Lance Corporal, looking harassed]

Lance Corporal:	He is still not back, king sir.
Abednego *[furiously]:*	Back from where? Speak, you fool!

Lance Corporal:	They say . . . . I was not there, king . . . . They came and told me . . .
Abednego:	Told you what, you idiot?
Lance Corporal:	King, it is what they told me . . . That it is the witch girl . . . . That she was running down to the stream . . . . She was running and running . . . down to the stream . . . . then Okpijo was running after her and shouting because of blood in his eye . . .
Abednego:	Blood in his eye?
Lance Corporal:	And knife, King sir . . .
Abednego:	You're a bastard! Always one useless report or another!
Lance Corporal:	No complain' sir, King!
Abednego *[indicating Echezo]:*	That idiot they call Echezona, he thinks he is being clever . . . . Take him away and reserve him for me. Nobody mocks me and nobody will waste my time with stupid talk. I know the white man was eaten and I know who ate him.

[Re-enter Sergeant, Hezekiah at his side]

Sergeant *[looking very worried]:*	King, sir . . . . something has happened . . .
Abednego:	Sergeant, my problem with you is: you are too slow! See how long it took you to arrest this idiot they call Hezekiah who wrote a big lie to Dio, talking about grave, grave! Which grave? When and where did you bury your dead master?
Sergeant:	King sir, there is something you need to hear . . . .
Abednego:	Keep out of this, Sergeant. What kind of king do you people want me to be? A costume and foofoo clown to be dribbled by every cockroach? A jester that goes out with goats and returns with rats? Did I not make it clear that I will never

shrink or retreat? I will break your cabal of evil and expose all you vultures who ate the body of the white preacher.

[The assembly had parted as he was speaking, allowing the four sons of Iwobi to set down their father's bamboo bed. The still figure on the bed slowly parts the coverlet and the boys lend him a hand. Gasps of incredulity and shouts of joy follow as a pallid frail-looking Rev Jones manages to sit up]

Abednego:	Ojongo!
Hezekiah:	Not Ojongo please. This is Reverend Jones!
Akaeze:	Umudimkpa, behold the white man . . . . the man that Akaeze and Orimili ate in the mouth of this . . . . this beast of no origin . . . .

[chokes and just shakes his head. Rev Jones is fondly mobbed]

Rev Jones *[weakly and hoarsely]:* Explain it to them, Hezekiah . . .

Hezekiah: It is God! It is the kindness of God that showed us the next day that he was still breathing . . . . so we arranged for special help.

Rev Jones *[hoarsely and slowly]:* Tell them to fear no one but God . . . . the owner of all creation . . . . He has preserved my life for the work that He wants me to do in this land. It is a work we shall do together for His glory . . . . . . Tell them to fear no guns . . . . The weapons of our warfare are not carnal, but mighty through God, to pull down strongholds.

[Tumult as Ebili re-enters with a bundle of brooms and everyone in the assembly grabs one]

Abednego *[in panic]:* Brooms, Ojongo! Br-o-ooooms!

[Broom in hand, all face Abednego and his gang who squeeze into the corner. Constable 1

pulls off his uniform, joins Ogbuefi Ekwegbalu in loosening the ropes on Orimili Obiora and then picks up a broom for himself. Ojongo backs away, muttering frantically into his rattles, Abednego and his troops crowding behind him in full retreat]

Orimili Obiora: We shall now arise and go up to the palace. We must clean it up and preserve it for the true king who will surely come . . . .

[Fade]

 EPILOGUE

Throne Room at the Umudimkpa palace, throne and high stools restored. Off-stage, Hezekiah and his class are chanting "A Man and a Pan". Sounds of applause follow . . . . Enter Ebili, a red-and-white nightcap on his head and a whitish cloth worn toga-wise over his ankle-length brown wrapper. He blows softly on his flute and narrates intermittently.

What Ebili saw, you too have seen
    And it fills the eye
What Ebili heard, you too have heard
    And it crowds the ear
If the tale is fire, may my head and yours
    Be no cheap faggot

Umudimkpa regained our palace
    by whisper of brooms,
By mere whisper of brooms
Not the bloody flash of matchets
The people only moved as one
And guns failed the bloody goon

I hear you ask: Where is Apiti?
Did you not hear? He escaped to the camp
To make that hole a fortress
A fortress of his fears . . . . his very own prison
And we pray, his grave

I wish I could say that we, the people
Were able to stop that coronation
But wishes at times are slippery like the eel
And some ugly ills cannot be wished away

His white friend came down one morning

- 197 -

Put paper in his hand, fancy cap on his head
Called him their chief of chiefs
And prisoners brought from far and wide
Danced and clapped for him
(For the next ration of measly beans
Engaged with soaked garri
A starving man will dance, forgive!)
And troops with loaded guns
Were brave against our goats

Umudimkpa in spite of orders
Stayed away as one, preferred to pay the fine
And we are still paying
The thieving claw of taxation pinching where it hurts

[Enter Echezo with a musical troupe. They promptly set up and play the first limbering note of Uri oma le, le, le!]

Echezo: That is the tune we learnt from his hired minstrel. All the way from Owerre, they meant it as an anthem, but it mocks him to the bones!

[Sings and dances with Ebili as the troupe plays]

Uri oma, leee, le, lee!
Uri oma
Urioma leee, le, lee!
Uri oma
Mu na nwannem gara ikpanku n'ugbo eze
Uri oma
Kpachaa nku ghara nwannem nkem lawa
Uri oma
Okporoko ijiji abiagh nga anyi n'echi eze
Uri oma
Onye anya mpia abiagh nga anyi n'echi eze
Uri oma!
Eze anyi chiri echichi bekee
Uri oma bekee, uri oma bekee, uri oma!

Ebili: He takes that song with him everywhere. A mockery of self but he doesn't seem to understand!

Echezo: That song reckons the new wave of selfishness and betrayals as a bragging right. Brother minds only his own firewood and abandons his dear brother in the bush, just to see a king crowned in the white man's style—a show of class, no houseflies, no one-eyed man!

Ebili: But who are his houseflies? The people he wants to rule? That fellow, Apiti is cursed for ever, a ruler without subjects!

Echezo: Big laugh on his strongman, Okpijo, the big bully. He too could not attend, his one good eye lost to the maid he defiled. He is dying a slow and painful death, polluting our ears with horrible confessions.

Ebili: But Akweke drowned herself, and her complete story drowned with her! This rape talk is a sorry ghost I wish they put away.

Echezo: The whole land is raped beyond proof! But you and I stand tall because we stood up! We took the shame, refusing to die like fools or hang like cowards . . . and we've denied evil a foothold in our palace.

Ebili: Brooms are all it took. Brooms, Echezo! And a bit of brains! No guns! No matchets! But we've taken back our palace. And we have our own white friend.

Echezo: Do you know what I love in that man? He is learning our language . . . . as we are learning his own . . . . You'll always hear from him *"Kunaaka! Kunaaka! Kunaaka!"*

> *[Enter Hezekiah, leading Iwobi's children and a few other pupils in a single file, all clapping. The musical troupe rises to join]*

Ebili: Victims of wrong are gifted with a choice
To wear it as a curse or fight it as a cause
To sink in gloom and despair, mourning for ever
Or rise to champion right, having paid the price
> *[Hezekiah leads a sing-song of 'A Man, A Pan, A Man and a Pan']*
Tomorrow is a prayer, this moment is our chance
We can rise to take the mountains for our children

Or sit and sulk our lifetime away in the ash of self-defeat . . .
> *[Joins the musical troupe with Echezo in escorting the dancing pupils all chanting and clapping, Hezekiah in the lead]*

The End.